DISCOVER
Geary County
KANSAS

**Nature, History, and Hometown
Hospitality in the Sunflower State**

THERESA L. GOODRICH

Contents

Introduction

Bite-sized guides; Buffet-sized adventures

WELCOME TO GEARY COUNTY, Kansas, a destination filled with nature, history, and hometown hospitality.

Every place has stories. It's my passion to bring them to life, and I've been doing this a very, very long time: in 2002, I founded The Local Tourist as a guide to one neighborhood in downtown Chicago. Today, I cover travel all over the United States, specializing in road trips, the great outdoors, and unique destinations. I'm also a publisher and author of multiple books, most of which are themed around travel. Even my fiction is travel-related: my protagonist is a travel writer.

I've created this guidebook in partnership with the Geary County Convention and Visitors Bureau. They pointed me in the right direction, introduced me to several of the people you'll meet in these pages, and covered my expenses. However, all opinions are expressly my own.

It's been my long-held belief that traveling to a place is not just about doing things. It's about truly experiencing a destination. Learning its stories. Meeting its residents. I want to help you go beyond the interstate and discover this welcome surprise.

In this guide, you'll find an array of things to do, with both extensive profiles of my favorite places and directory-style listings to round out your planning.

> **TLTip:** Throughout this guide, you'll see this term. It's to highlight a quick tip and is a play on the initials of my website, **The Local Tourist**.

I hope this guide helps you experience the fascination of a tourist while feeling the comfort of the local.

Enjoy the journey and have fun being a Local Tourist!

Theresa Goodrich

Welcome to Geary County, Kansas

A land of open sky, open water, and open opportunities

AS A LIFELONG MIDWESTERNER (with the exception of one brief four-year stint), I'm familiar with the phrase "flyover country." Lots of people seem to think there's nothing to do around here.

I understand why it can seem like that, especially if you're driving I-80 through Iowa and Nebraska and I-70 through Illinois and Kansas. I still remember a family trip to Colorado from Indiana when I was 14. Without cell phones, smart phones, tablets, DVD players, podcasts, satellite radio, or any of those other distractions that are so prevalent today, my brother and I were left with Mad Libs, reading, and picking on each other.

I spent a lot of time looking out the window, wondering what went on beyond the billboards. As I've learned during my years as a travel writer, there are more stories than I could tell in a lifetime.

If you stay on the highways, it seems like the Midwest in general and the Sunflower State in particular are a whole lotta nothin'. But when you take those exits, you discover there's a lot more happening.

Not that there are suddenly booming metropolises along the two-lanes. Those small towns and those wide open spaces are part of the charm, part of the defining reason to get off the highway and slow down for a bit.

Geary County, Kansas, is one of those places that's accused of being a bit, shall we say, sleepy. And by some definitions, it is. Which is why it makes a perfect place for a relaxing getaway, one filled with outdoor fun, history, and a whole lot of hospitality.

Or as we call it, "Midwest nice."

Geary County straddles I-70 and is probably most well-known as the gateway to Fort Riley and the home of Milford Lake, a destination for fishing enthusiasts. But beyond the Army base and the state's largest lake, Geary County offers a blend of natural beauty and small-town charm that might surprise you. But what's even more surprising is the pivotal role this area played in American history.

This region was at the heart of the struggle against slavery in the mid-19th century. As part of "Bleeding Kansas," Geary County and its surroundings were instrumental in the fight to make Kansas a free state, and are why it's included in the Freedom's Frontier National Heritage Area. The passion and principles of those early settlers helped shape not just the state, but the nation's trajectory towards abolition.

The ideals that made this region crucial in the fight against slavery helped shape the Geary County of today. It's a welcoming community that, despite being the second smallest county in Kansas, is the third most diverse.

DISCOVER GEARY COUNTY

This diversity is evident in its varied food scene. While you'll find classic Midwestern fare, you can also enjoy a range of international cuisines that might seem unexpected in the heart of Kansas.

History buffs will find plenty to explore, with several museums detailing Geary County's military past, and there are sites offering windows into different eras of Kansas history.

If you're a nature lover, there are lots of opportunities to connect with the outdoors. This land of prairie and Flint Hills is the Fishing Capital of Kansas and also draws avid hunters, birdwatchers, and hikers.

In this guide, we'll explore this fascinating county in the northeastern part of Kansas. You'll learn the stories behind the towns of Geary County, including the not one, not two, but four attempts to build a town where Junction City now stands.

And because reading about a place is great, but visiting is even better, you'll find practical guidance on things to do. There are activities for outdoor adventurers, historical attractions, and a community that's dedicated to proving that being nice can mean finishing first. You'll also find nearby attractions so you can extend your stay.

We'll start with some things to know before you go: e.g. weather, location, time zone, etc. Before we get into the nitty gritty of planning your visit, you'll find answers to your FAQs, and then it's a brief dive into the area's complex past, because to understand a destination's past is to appreciate its present. There are in-depth profiles of my favorite places, and more directory-style listings of things to do, places to eat, and where to stay.

Because this is a guide to help you *plan* your vacation to Geary County, there are itinerary planning pages. And, to help you remember your experience long after you've returned to the chaos of daily life, there's also space to record your memories.

Geary County offers a unique blend of experiences. It's a place where you can slow down and discover the often-overlooked charms of the American Midwest, and in the following pages, you'll discover the attractions, activities, and hospitality that make Geary County special.

Enough chit-chat. Are you ready to Discover Geary County?

Know Before You Go

Important details for planning your trip

BEFORE YOU HEAD TO Geary County, there are a few essential details that will help you navigate your way through these north central Kansas communities. Here's a snapshot of what to expect.

Location

Geary County straddles I-70 and is about an hour west of Topeka, Kansas, and less than two hours north-northeast of Wichita.

Transportation

The nearest major airport is Manhattan Regional Airport (MHK), about 20 minutes east of Junction City. Kansas City International Airport (MCI) is approximately 2.5 hours away. Within Geary County, personal vehicles are the primary mode of transportation, though limited public transit options are available in Junction City.

Time Zone

Geary County is in the Central Time Zone and follows Daylight Savings Time.

Population

As of the 2020 Census, Geary County had a population of 36,779 people. Two-thirds of them live in Junction City.

Weather

Geary County experiences a Midwestern climate with four distinct seasons. Summers are often hot and humid, while winters can be cold with occasional snowfall.

- Spring: Mild with temperatures ranging from mid-forties to upper seventies.

- Summer: Temperatures often soar into the upper eighties and nineties, often with days exceeding one hundred degrees. Humidity is high, making it feel even hotter.

- Fall: This season brings a drop in temperatures, ranging from the sixties to the low eighties early in the season, and then cooling down to the forties by November. The weather is generally dry with clear skies.

- Winter: Winters can be chilly, with average temperatures ranging from the twenties to forties. Snowfall is moderate, and cold fronts can bring frigid air from the north, leading to lower temperatures at times.

Best Time to Visit

- Spring: Expect wildflowers, mild weather, great bird-watching, and fantastic fishing.

- Summer: Enjoy water activities, camping, outdoor concerts, and vibrant Fourth of July celebrations.

- Fall: Experience stunning fall foliage, harvest festivals, cool hikes, and historic tours.

- Winter: Perfect for a cozy getaway, especially if you enjoy snow-related activities.

Language

English is the primary language, though you may hear multiple languages because of the diversity of the county's residents.

Currency

The U.S. Dollar (USD) is the currency used. Credit cards are widely accepted, but it's wise to carry some cash, particularly when visiting farmers markets.

Tipping

Tipping is customary in the United States, including in Geary County. Here are some general guidelines:

- Restaurants: 15-20% of the pre-tax bill is standard for sit-down service. For exceptional service, 20-25% is appreciated.

- Bars: $1-2 per drink or 15-20% of the total bill.

- Taxis/Rideshares: 15-20% of the fare.

- Hotel housekeeping: $2-5 per night, left daily.

- Barbers/Hairdressers: 15-20% of the service cost.

- Food delivery: 10-15% of the order total.

Note that some restaurants may add an automatic gratuity for large groups. Always check your bill to avoid double-tipping.

Dress Code

Casual and comfortable attire is appropriate.

Parking

Parking is readily available and free in most areas of Geary County. In downtown Junction City, there are both on-street parking spaces and public lots. Always check for any posted time limits or restrictions.

Alcohol Laws

The legal drinking age in Kansas is 21. Alcohol sales are permitted between 9 AM and 11 PM Monday through Saturday, and 12 PM to 8 PM on Sundays. Some restaurants may have different serving hours. Open container laws are enforced, so avoid consuming alcohol in public spaces.

Beer is available at some grocery stores. All other liquor, including wine, can be purchased at dedicated liquor stores.

Cell Phone Coverage

Cell phone coverage is generally good throughout Geary County, especially in and around Junction City. However, some rural areas may have spotty coverage. Major carriers like Verizon, AT&T, and T-Mobile provide service in the area.

Emergency Services

For emergencies, dial 911. The primary healthcare facility is Stormont Vail Health - Flint Hills Campus, 1102 St. Mary's Road, Junction City. For non-emergency police matters, call 785-238-4131.

Special Events and Festivals

Check the local calendar for events such as seasonal festivals, and unique cultural experiences.

Visit Geary County

Don't forget to check out the voice of authority on all things Geary County. The Geary County Convention and Visitors Bureau offers a wealth of information, and it's their passion to help you find things to do. Check out their website at visitgearycounty.com. Once you're in the area, say hi. Their visitor center is at 222 W 6th Street, Junction City, KS 66441 800-528-2489.

Visiting Fort Riley FAQs

THERE ARE SEVERAL MUSEUMS within Fort Riley, but since this is an active military base, you can't just walk up to the door. Here's what you need to know before you go.

Q: How can I visit the museums at Fort Riley?
A: Visitors need to obtain a pass from the Visitor Control Center, located near Henry Gate at Exit 301 off I-70. U.S. citizens can get a short-term pass with proper identification. International visitors may need to apply in advance.

Q: I'm a U.S. citizen. What identification do I need to enter Fort Riley?
A: U.S. citizens need a government-issued photo ID (Driver's License, state ID, passport, foreign passport w/ VISA, resident alien).

Q: Are there guided tours available of Fort Riley?
A: There are no guided tours of Fort Riley, but there are self-guided driving and walking tours. Check Fort Riley Historical Society's website (fortrileyhistoricalsociety.org/) for information.

Q: Which museums can I visit at Fort Riley?
A: Fort Riley has several museums open to the public, including

the U.S. Cavalry Museum and the 1st Infantry Division Museum. The historic Custer House is also open for tours. Check the Historical Attractions chapter for details.

Q: Are there any restrictions on photography in the museums or during tours?
A: Photography is generally allowed in the museums and on tours for personal use. However, always check with museum staff about any specific restrictions.

Q: Can visitors eat at restaurants on the base?
A: Yes, there are dining facilities on base that are open to visitors at the Exchange. Be sure to keep your visitor's pass with you.

Q: What are the operating hours for the museums and tours?
A: Hours can vary seasonally. It's best to check the Fort Riley website or call the Visitor Center for current hours of operation. 785-239-2982 home.army.mil/riley/index.php/about/visitor-info

Q: Is there a dress code for visiting the museums or taking tours?
A: While there's no strict dress code, it's recommended to dress comfortably and modestly. Remember, you're visiting an active military installation.

Q: Can I bring my bag/backpack into the museums?
A: Small bags are usually allowed, but they may be subject to search. Large backpacks or bags might need to be stored or left in your vehicle.

Q: Are the museums and tours wheelchair accessible?
A: Many areas are wheelchair accessible, but it's best to check in advance for specific accommodations, especially for historic buildings.

Remember to verify this information with Fort Riley's official sources, as policies can change. You might also want to include contact information for Fort Riley's Visitor Control Center or Public Affairs Office for those seeking the most up-to-date information. 785-239-2982 home.army.mil/riley/index.php/about/visitor-info

How Geary County Came to Be

GEARY COUNTY'S MOTTO SEEMS to be if at first you don't succeed, try, try again. Today it's an example of community pride and small town success, but its early years were met with challenges. Things like a bogus legislature, a bogus town, unscrupulous speculators, pro-slavery forces, and a community destroyed by a Secretary of War could have spelled certain doom. Instead, the people of what was then the frontier met each problem head-on, and when one solution didn't work, they'd find another.

In the mid-1800s, more and more Americans packed their belongings in wagons and left their homes in search of something better. Following the Oregon-California or the Santa Fe Trails, both of which began in Missouri, they headed west with everything they could carry.

The U.S. Government began providing military escorts to protect them, and they also built forts for the same reason. In the fall of 1852, a captain in the 1st U.S. Dragoons surveyed the junction where the Smoky Hill and Republican Rivers join to form the Kansas. It was a perfect spot for a garrison. Initially named Camp Center because it was believed to be near the geographical center of the country, it was changed to Fort Riley in 1853. This name change honored Maj. Gen. Bennett C. Riley, who had led the first military escort on the Santa Fe Trail in 1829.

Although the first buildings were constructed of wood, they quickly began using the local limestone, giving Fort Riley its distinctive architectural character. Captain Edmund Ogden supervised this early construction, but was one of many victims of a cholera epidemic in 1855. Within the fort, two monuments honor his contribution, and the town of Ogden at the fort's eastern gate is named for him.

Another victim of 1855 was the town of Pawnee. This small settlement on the Kansas River sprang up after it was announced in September 1854 that the territory's new legislature would convene near Fort Riley.

During these early years, the country was a powder keg as pro- and anti-slavery forces battled. Not only did soldiers garrisoned at Fort Riley have to increasingly patrol the Santa Fe Trail, they also had to act as peacemakers between the warring factions. The

Kansas-Nebraska Act of 1854 dictated that popular sovereignty would decide whether Kansas would be a free state or not: it was up to the territory's settlers. The people who'd established the town of Pawnee were overwhelmingly free-staters. The politicians, however, were not.

Governor Andrew Reeder opposed slavery, but the lawmakers didn't care. The sessions began on July 2, 1855, and by July 4 they'd passed a resolution to move the seat of government to Shawnee Mission, which was close to the Missouri border. That made it easier for residents of Missouri, a slave state since its founding in 1821, to cross into Kansas Territory and pretend to be locals so they could influence the vote. Governor Reeder vetoed the measure, but the bogus legislature, as it would become known, overrode him. The First Territorial Capitol of Kansas lasted all of five days.

By September of that year, Secretary of War Jefferson Davis, who would become the President of the Confederacy, expanded the borders of Fort Riley to encompass Pawnee, destroying the town, which by that time had reached a population of around 500. The capitol is the only building that remains.

That same summer, the first attempt to build a town were Junction City now stands began. Four agents of the Cincinnati-Manhattan Company staked out a town site at the junction of the Republican and Smoky Hill Rivers. They named it Manhattan, then followed the Kansas River downstream to meet their company's steamboat, the Hartford, for supplies. Low water levels prevented the boat from going upstream beyond the mouth of the Blue River, and when the agents reached the confluence, realized there was already a town. The agents negotiated with the residents, got half the town site, and named it Manhattan instead.

After unloading the Hartford and freeing it from the sandbar, the steamboat's Captain Millard decided to continue upstream. He moved the original Manhattan site, although it was still at the junction, and named it Millard City. This new town got a little further, forming the Cincinnati-Kansas Manufacturing Company with ten members on October 3, 1855. They began building a hotel, digging a cellar and stocking lumber, but that winter the lumber "somehow disappeared for some debts due," according to an article in the Junction City Union of February 19, 1870.

Lumber wasn't the only thing that disappeared. The Company drew up a plat and began selling lots back east, taking in anywhere between $40,000 and $100,000, although there were no records. The money never made it back to Millard City, and the two agents left to manage it ended up abandoning the site.

The third attempt was made in the summer of 1857 by farmers who'd settled in the area, but the furthest they got was giving it the name of Humboldt.

Then, finally, in October of that year, a group of settlers, including some of those who'd tried to establish Humboldt, successfully established the town of Junction City. Surveying began in December and was completed in the spring of 1858, with the first building erected in May near present day Washington and Seventh.

When the bogus legislature convened for those five days in 1855, they also created Riley County and Davis County, named for Jefferson Davis. Although originally both governed from Riley County, in 1857 Davis County became a separate corporation and in 1860, Junction City became the county seat.

Residents of Davis County were primarily free-staters. Once the Civil War started and Davis became the president of the confederacy, the idea of having their county named for him rankled. They tried to change it to Lyon County in 1862, but another county had taken that. Then in 1864, they wanted Lincoln County, with the same result. Finally, more than two decades later, the name officially changed to Geary County on February 28, 1889. The new name honored General John White Geary, who had been the third Territorial Governor of Kansas and a Union War hero.

Communities of Geary County

Meet the Communities

GEARY COUNTY, KANSAS, COMPRISES four communities: Junction City, Grandview Plaza, Milford, and Fort Riley, an active U.S. Army base. While a small portion of the fort is within the county lines, its presence has a significant impact.

At only 384.7 square miles, the county is the second smallest in the state. However, it's also the second or third most diverse, depending on the source. As you explore, you'll see evidence of this diversity everywhere you go, especially in the varieties of cuisine.

Here's a brief overview of each community.

Junction City

Junction City is the largest city in Geary County and serves as the county seat. The fourth attempt at establishing a community on this site, it's the town that almost wasn't. The first three tries were washouts, with one being nothing more than a paper town. Finally, in 1858, Junction City stuck, named for its position at the junction of the Republican and Smoky Hill rivers.

The city's history and development is intertwined with Fort Riley's. Junction City became a key hub during westward expansion, with its location on the Smoky Hill Trail and the military presence of the nearby fort driving its early growth.

Today, Junction City boasts a variety of historical and cultural attractions. The C.L. Hoover Opera House, originally built in 1882 and restored in 2008, is a cornerstone of the local arts scene, hosting performances ranging from community theater to orchestras. Meanwhile, Rathert Stadium, a Depression-era project, continues to be a cherished venue for baseball fans, and it's home to the multi-championship winning team, the Junction City Brigade. There are in-depth profiles of both these attractions, and more, in this book.

In addition to its deep historical roots, Junction City is home to the nearby Milford Lake, the largest man-made lake in Kansas, where residents and visitors enjoy boating, fishing, and hiking. The city also connects with the natural beauty of the region through the Riverwalk Trail, which extends from Milford Lake to Fort Riley, offering picturesque views of the Republican River and the chance to see wildlife such as bald eagles.

Junction City's economy remains closely tied to Fort Riley, and the town's welcoming attitude toward military families is apparent in its amenities and community events. The presence of Fort Riley continues to influence the local economy, culture, and even the demographics, with a significant portion of the population either serving in the military or having a family member stationed at the fort.

Fort Riley

Fort Riley, established in 1853, was named after Major General Bennett C. Riley. It was initially founded to protect settlers and travelers on the Santa Fe Trail and to defend the Western frontier. The fort's location along the Kansas River made it a strategic point for military operations in the region.

Over the years, Fort Riley became a central training ground for cavalry and infantry units. One of its most notable historical roles was serving as the home of the U.S. Army Cavalry School, which was instrumental in training cavalry forces before mechanization took hold in the mid-20th century. It was also home to the 9th and 10th Cavalry – the Buffalo Soldiers, African American soldiers who served in segregated regiments after the Civil War.

Today, Fort Riley is home to the 1st Infantry Division, also known as "The Big Red One," one of the oldest and most decorated divisions in the U.S. Army. The division has participated in numerous military operations, from World War I to modern conflicts.

While it's an active military base, parts of Fort Riley are open to the public, offering a fascinating glimpse into military life past and present through its museums and historic sites. *Visit the Fort Riley chapter for more information.*

Grandview Plaza

Grandview Plaza is a small community just east of Junction City. It's situated along Interstate 70, making it easily accessible to travelers passing through the region. The town was incorporated in 1963, but was mentioned as early as 1951 as a new development. An early business was "Cohen's Chicken House," a spot that had received national attention. After several floods at its original Junction City location, the restaurant moved to Grandview Plaza in 1952. When the city incorporated, Sammy Cohen became its first mayor.

While the Chicken House closed in 1993, there's another spot that's still open. Stacy's Restaurant has been serving "good home cookin'" since 1969 and is still a local favorite.

Milford

Milford, originally known as Bacheller, is a tiny town with a knack for reinvention. Founded in 1855 as Bacheller, it later adopted the name Milford in 1868. The town's location changed too - it was moved to higher ground in the 1960s due to the creation of Milford Lake.

Perhaps Milford's most salacious claim to fame was a man named John R. Brinkley, a notorious figure in medical history. After moving to Milford in 1917, Brinkley opened a small clinic the following year. Although initially successful, he decided to expand his practice with a highly controversial and unorthodox treatment. Brinkley claimed to cure male fertility issues by surgically implanting goat testicles into men.

Yes, you read that right.

Obviously, it didn't work, but not before attracting patients from across the country, many of whom found him because of the radio station he'd founded as an advertising tool. This made Brinkley a wealthy man, so much so that he paid for several improvements to the town, including a new sewage system, sidewalks, a bandstand, and electricity. It took several years, but his shady practices caught up with him. He ended up penniless, dying in San Antonio in 1942.

Exploring
Geary County

Overview

NOW THAT YOU'VE LEARNED about Geary County's fascinating past and have met the communities of this vibrant area, it's time to start exploring. The following sections will make it easy to plan, and will introduce you to several of the locals who make this area so welcoming.

In Hometown Hospitality, you'll discover Junction City's hospitality and its exponential growth. With the many **Historical Attractions**, you'll go deeper into the past and see for yourself the stories that made this area what it is. And since one of the main draws of this area is **The Great Outdoors**, make sure you explore the natural beauty of the prairies and the Flint Hills. The **Dining** section will give you an overview of the area's culinary options, with suggestions for several local restaurants. And in Annual Events, you'll find festivities you'll want to add to your own calendar.

Looking to see what else is nearby? Check **Extend Your Trip** for suggestions on day trips from Geary County. Don't miss **Where to Stay** for lodging ideas, and when you're ready to start putting it all together, use the resources in **Plan Your Adventure**.

Are you ready to explore Geary County? Let's go!

Top Things to Do in Geary County

1. Catch a show at the C.L. Hoover Opera House: Experience live performances in a beautifully restored historic venue dating back to 1882.

2. Explore the Geary County Historical Museum: Delve into local history through exhibits showcasing the area's development from frontier days to present.

3. Scream for ice cream at Hildebrand Farms Dairy: Enjoy farm-fresh dairy products, including delicious ice cream, at this family-owned dairy dating back to the 1930s.

4. Attend a Junction City Brigade baseball game at Rathert Stadium: Cheer on the local summer collegiate baseball team in a historic limestone stadium built in 1937.

5. Fish to your heart's content at Milford Lake: Cast a line in Kansas' largest man-made lake, known as the "Fishing Capital of Kansas."

6. Visit the Fort Riley Museums and Monuments: Explore military history at the U.S. Cavalry Museum and 1st Infantry Division Museum on this historic army post.

7. Hike or bike the Riverwalk Trail along the Republican River: Enjoy scenic views and wildlife along this paved trail connecting Milford Lake to Fort Riley.

8. Support local artisans at the Main Street Market: Browse handcrafted goods and local produce at this community market in downtown Junction City.

9. Play a round of golf at Rolling Meadows Golf Course: Tee off at this 18-hole public course offering beautiful views of the Flint Hills.

10. Explore the Konza Prairie Biological Station: Hike through pristine tallgrass prairie and experience the unique ecosystem of the Flint Hills.

11. Visit Heritage Park and its monuments: Discover local history through various monuments and markers in this downtown Junction City park.

12. Go birdwatching at Geary State Fishing Lake and Wildlife Area: Spot diverse bird species in this tranquil setting popular with nature enthusiasts.

13. Take a self-guided tour of Junction City's public art: Admire murals, sculptures, and other public artworks that showcase the city's culture and history.

14. Visit the Milford Nature Center & Fish Hatchery: Learn about local wildlife and fish production at this educational center near Milford Lake.

15. Explore shops and restaurants in downtown Junction City: Experience small-town charm while browsing local busi-

nesses and eateries.

16. Visit the Buffalo Soldiers Memorial: Pay tribute to the African American cavalry units that served at Fort Riley at this meaningful monument.

17. Follow the Black History Trail of Geary County: Learn about the contributions of African Americans to the area's development through various historical sites.

18. Get a close-up look at an Atomic Cannon: View this unique Cold War-era weapon, one of the largest artillery pieces ever built, at Fort Riley.

19. Sleep in a yurt at Acorns Resort: Enjoy a unique glamping experience in these circular tents on the shores of Milford Lake.

20. Tour a world of cuisine in one Kansas city: Sample diverse international cuisines reflecting Junction City's multicultural population and military connections.

Geary County Outdoors

Muralist: Chase Hunter
Base Sponsor: Geary County
Convention & Visitors Bureau

Hometown Hospitality

Overview

WELCOME TO JUNCTION CITY, where "Midwest Nice" is front and center and community pride is clear. While the county seat has been through some rough times, it's rebounded and is now an example of revitalization.

When you visit Junction City, you'll see that community pride in its public art and the preservation of its past, the celebration of its present, and the hope for its future.

In 2020, the community applied for the Main Street America program and participation has made a significant difference. Check out **Spotlight on Main Street** for this inspiring success story.

Hildebrand Farms Dairy is another success. This family-owned business has been around since the 1930s, surviving the many upheavals in farming, and it began with a swoon-worthy love story.

And no mention of Junction City's success would be complete without including the JC Brigade. This collegiate baseball team won seven out of ten championships between 2014, when the Mid-Plains League was formed, and 2024. Talk about a winning record!

Let's experience some of that Hometown Hospitality, shall we?

Spotlight on Main Street

A Small Town Success Story

JUNCTION CITY, KANSAS, IS a vibrant community that is a model of small-town success stories. Beginning in 2020, Junction City embarked on an ambitious transformation, breathing new life into its downtown, fostering a thriving business environment, and creating a sense of place that resonates with both long-time residents and newcomers alike.

Terry Butler, Vice President of the Junction City Main Street Board of Directors and a passionate advocate for Junction City's revitalization, captured the spirit of this transformation:

"There is a movement in Junction City," Terry said. "And I'm telling you, it is not going to end. It is just beginning, and it makes me cry. It's unbelievable. It's just unbelievable."

I spoke with multiple people during my time in Geary County, and her sentiment was echoed throughout the community.

From the installation of eye-catching statues to the farmers and makers markets that showcase local producers, Junction City's story is one of community collaboration, innovative thinking, and a deep-seated belief in the potential of this place where the Smoky Hill and Republican rivers meet.

This is a community on the rise with, as Terry put it, "a uniquely American story."

The Main Street Program

Junction City's remarkable transformation is largely attributed to its participation in the Main Street America program.

Founded by the National Trust for Historic Preservation in 1977, this program works with governmental organizations and corporations, providing access to grants, educational support, and more for historic downtowns. As one of only twelve accredited Main Street communities in Kansas, the city has come together to reimagine its urban core.

The Main Street America program provides a proven framework for community-driven, comprehensive growth. Junction City embraced this approach, following the program's four-point strategy:

- Promotion

- Design

- Organization

- Economic Vitality

Junction City began the process in 2020. Everything was shut down, so they had time to think about the future. It's clear this transformation didn't happen because of a handful of people. City and county officials, organizations, and individuals had meeting after meeting, trying to figure out what they could do to improve their home.

That commitment was evident in their fundraising efforts: in about two months, a team almost completely comprised of volunteers raised almost a half million dollars.

After months of planning, they applied and were accredited in 2021. Once a community receives accreditation, it's not a done deal: they must resubmit annually, and Junction City is now in its third year.

The impact of the Main Street program on Junction City has been profound, adding eighteen new businesses by the summer of 2024.

Creating a Vibrant Downtown

Downtown revitalization has been at the heart of Junction City's transformation. Infrastructure improvements, new businesses, and public art initiatives have breathed new life into the city center.

Two of these initiatives focus on public art. If you stroll around Junction City, you'll see several "JC statues." These tell the story of Junction City through art. There are also multiple murals, many by in-demand artist Mindy Allen. She's a local who, through her company Mindy's Murals, is known for her vibrant paintings.

One of the most impactful is the "Come Together" mural. While Mindy designed it, the community literally came together to paint it.

There are also all those new businesses. One of those is Highwind Brewing Company. A collaboration of many local investors and business people, it's in an historic building that had been empty for decades. After a multi-million dollar renovation, it's now a new favorite watering hole with food hall-style dining.

Community Events

Community events didn't start with Main Street participation, but they've played a crucial role in driving the growth of Junction City.

Freedom Fest, a five-day celebration that draws 40,000 to 50,000 people, showcases Junction City over the Independence Day holiday.

The Oktoberfest celebration has seen exponential growth. "The first year, we hoped for 1000 but we had 4000," Terry said. "The second year, we hoped for 10,000, planned for 12,000, had 14,000. And the third year we had 15 to 20,000."

Other events like Paint the Town Blue parade and Hometown Christmas have quickly become beloved traditions, fostering community pride and attracting visitors.

Supporting Local Entrepreneurs

Supporting local entrepreneurs has been a key aspect of Junction City's strategy. The city has developed programs like JCE 101 (Junction City Entrepreneur 101) and JCE 201 to support aspiring business owners, particularly those connected to Fort Riley.

There are several home-based businesses in Fort Riley, and with these resources, Junction City can help them be set up for success.

Leveraging Natural Resources

Junction City is also looking to capitalize on its natural resources. As the home of the largest lake in Kansas and the fishing capital of the state, Geary County offers several opportunities for outside adventures.

Plans are underway to tap into these resources more effectively, including involvement in the Kansas Gravel Initiative to promote biking routes.

What's Next for Junction City

Looking to the future, Terry outlined several key areas for Junction City's continued growth, including downtown recreation, outdoor dining, and mixed-use housing. The "Gate to Gate Rejuvenate" project aims to improve the corridor between Fort Riley and downtown Junction City, further integrating the military community with the city.

To ensure the sustainability of these efforts, new initiatives like "Flags of Geary County" are being implemented. This program, inspired by a similar initiative in Texarkana, will serve as a fundraiser for Main Street while engaging various community groups in its execution.

As Junction City continues to grow and evolve, it stands as a model for other small cities looking to improve their communities. The story of Junction City is one of resilience, innovation, and community spirit - a testament to what can be achieved when a town comes together with a shared vision for a brighter future.

For those looking to experience this transformation firsthand, Junction City invites you to visit and be part of its ongoing renaissance.

For more information, visit junctioncitymainstreet.com.

Public Art in Junction City

ONE OF THE WAYS Junction City celebrates its culture is through its commitment to public art. From monuments to murals, the city's streets and parks are decorated with visual representations of its history, diversity, and community spirit.

The Geary County Visitor's Guide has a map of murals and sculptures. *visitgearycounty.com*

JC Statues

As you walk around downtown, you can't miss the JC Statues. These artists' renditions of Junction City's heritage tell its story.

The first of the ten sculptures, which honors veterans, was unveiled in Heritage Park on September 8, 2022. Others celebrate agriculture, the arts, the outdoors, and the city's origins. One is dedicated to the community's diversity, and another to Big Red One.

These statues have been rolled out with great fanfare. When they revealed the Railroad and Cattle Drive statue, the town held a literal cattle drive up Washington Street.

Monuments

Heritage Park, in the heart of downtown, serves as an outdoor museum. Its collection of monuments and markers commemorates various aspects of Junction City and Geary County's history, from military service to pioneer spirit.

Other monuments include the Buffalo Soldiers statue at 18th Street and Buffalo Soldier Drive. It pays tribute to the 9th and 10th US Cavalry units that served at nearby Fort Riley.

One monument worth seeing, although it's not historically accurate, is in Coronado Park and dedicated to the Spaniard's expedition into Kansas in 1541. The monument was originally unveiled in 1902 by Captain Robert Henderson on his farm, complete with a national salute fired by a battery from Fort Riley. At the time, it was thought that Quivira, Coronado's destination, was located in Junction City. While the explorer did make it to Kansas, the legendary territory was actually further south in the state.

Murals

Murals are a delightful way to beautify urban spaces, and Junction City has embraced this art form in a big way. Many of the murals are by in-demand artist Mindy Allen. She's a local who, through her company Mindy's Murals, is known for her vibrant paintings. The Junction City Little Theater mural, created by artist Dr. Bob Palmer, honors the longest running community theater program in Kansas.

One of the most impactful of Mindy's Murals is "Come Together." While Mindy designed it, the community literally came together to paint it.

These public art installations do more than beautify the cityscape. They foster community pride, spark conversations, and provide a unique way for residents and visitors to connect with Junction City's past and present.

Geary Community Markets

GEARY COUNTY OFFERS TWO vibrant community markets that show-case local produce, handcrafted goods, and the area's entrepre-neurial spirit. These markets not only provide fresh, local prod-ucts but also serve as social hubs where residents and visitors can connect with local producers and artisans.

Geary Community Farmers Market

The Geary Community Farmers Market brings local farmers and artisans together to offer their freshest produce and handmade goods.

Visitors can find an array of seasonal fruits and vegetables. The market also features local honey, baked goods, and homemade preserves. Besides edibles, many vendors offer handcrafted items such as soaps, candles, and jewelry.

The Thursday evening timing makes this market a perfect after-work stop for many residents, creating a lively community atmosphere. It's not uncommon to see families strolling between stalls, sampling local delicacies, and chatting with the farmers about their growing methods.

For current schedule and location, visit livewellgearycounty.org.

Main Street Market

The Main Street Market focuses on showcasing the work of local artisans and craftspeople. This market is a treasure trove for those seeking unique, handcrafted items.

Visitors can expect to find a diverse range of products. Many of the vendors are happy to discuss their creative processes, making the market an interactive experience for those interested in the crafts.

There are food trucks on-site at this market, so come hungry. Also fun is the monthly Junk in the Trunk. Everyone's invited to bring whatever they've got to sell for a small fee.

For current schedule and location, visit junctioncitymainstreet. org.

Both markets not only provide fresh, local products and unique handcrafted items, but they also play a crucial role in supporting local businesses and fostering a sense of community. They offer a glimpse into the rich agricultural heritage and creative spirit of Geary County, making them must-visit attractions for anyone looking to experience the true flavor of the area.

Hildebrand Farms Dairy

Agritourism with a swoon-worthy love story

AT HILDEBRAND FARMS DAIRY in Junction City, the cream really does rise to the top. This family-owned operation offers more than just dairy products; it provides a taste of Kansas's rich agricultural heritage and a glimpse into the future of sustainable, local food production.

Since Arnold Hildebrand obtained his first permit to sell milk on September 15, 1930, this working dairy farm has been a family-owned staple. Today the farm is run by the third generation of Hildebrands: brothers David and Alan and their wives, Kathy and Mary.

Mary gave me a tour of their farm and told me its story. It's a tale of perseverance, innovation, and a deep commitment to quality, and it began with a bouquet of edelweiss.

A Swiss Love Story: The Dairy's Origins

In the 1920s, a young woman named Rosa left her home in Zurich and sailed across the Atlantic to America. She found work as a babysitter, leaving behind a suitor named Arnold.

Arnold, however, wasn't content to let the Atlantic Ocean come between them. Instead, he sold his sailboat so he could book passage to come to America. It's the kind of romantic gesture usually reserved for movies, but Arnold wasn't finished. When he arrived in America, he proposed to Rosa with a bouquet of edelweiss that he had picked in the Swiss mountains before his journey.

"We still have that all pressed in a little frame," Mary said.

The young couple eventually made their way to Kansas, settling in Junction City in the late 1920s. Arnold started a small dairy, laying the foundation for what would become Hildebrand Farms Dairy.

This Swiss-American love story set in motion a family legacy that has endured for nearly a century. From those humble beginnings, with Arnold and Rosa milking a small herd of cows, the Hildebrand dairy has grown into a local institution, known for its quality products and commitment to educating the public about dairy farming.

Family Legacy

The small dairy started by Arnold and Rosa grew, nurtured by the hard work and dedication of subsequent generations. Their son Carl, along with his wife Margaret, took over the operation in the mid-20th century, ushering in a new era of growth and innovation.

In the 1970s, Carl and Margaret faced a pivotal decision that many family farms encounter: expand or sell. They chose to expand, moving the dairy operation to its current location and building a new milking parlor in 1974.

Margaret, in particular, played a crucial role in keeping the farm going. "Really, she's the matriarch," Mary said. "I always tell people and I tell the family, if grandma hadn't stuck it out, we would not have been here."

At 97 years old, Margaret still drives out to the farm daily to check on operations.

Carl and Margaret's sons, Alan and Dave, continued to build on their parents' legacy. Mary remembered the early days:

"When I first got married {in 1988}, I think they were milking 60 cows, 70 cows. And I remember when we reached 100, that was a big milestone."

Today, the farm milks about 135 to 150 cows. The herd has grown, but the Hildebrand's commitment to quality and family values remains unchanged.

As with many family businesses, the next generation is already involved. Mary and Alan's two oldest children work on the farm, and Dave and Kathy's daughter and son are also part of the operation. This involvement of the younger generation ensures that the Hildebrand legacy will continue well into the future.

"We hope it's a legacy that continues long after we're gone," Mary said.

The Hildebrand story is more than just a tale of a successful business; it's a narrative of family perseverance, adaptability, and an unwavering commitment to their craft.

Expansion and Modernization

As the new millennium approached, the Hildebrand family once again found themselves at a crossroads. The dairy industry was changing rapidly, and small family farms were becoming increasingly rare. "There used to be many dairies in this county alone," Mary said, "and now I believe we're the only dairy in the county."

Faced with the choice to expand or sell, the Hildebrands chose a bold path forward. In the early 2000s, they decided to not only continue dairy farming but to venture into processing and bottling their own milk products.

This decision wasn't made lightly. Mary and Alan, along with Dave and his wife Kathy, visited small creameries around the country, gleaning what they could from their experiences. What they found was both enlightening and sobering.

"We started traveling and going to all these little creameries, you know, and just kind of doing our own research. And it's crazy because everyone we asked, would you do this again? Oh, no. We would not do this again."

Despite the cautionary tales, the Hildebrands pressed on. They had a feasibility study conducted, which showed promise for their venture. They also had a track record of quality to build upon — when selling their milk to larger companies like Blue Bunny, they consistently ranked in the top 5% for low bacteria counts.

The expansion included building a new processing plant and bottling facility on the farm. This allowed them to control the entire process from cow to consumer, ensuring the highest quality at every step.

It wasn't an easy transition. As Mary put it, "You just have to have faith, and it just becomes your way of life, actually." The learning curve was steep, and the work was demanding, but their persistence paid off. They secured contracts with major grocery chains like Kroger (operating as Dillons in Kansas) and expanded their reach across the state. They also opened a farm store, allowing them to sell directly to consumers and offer a wider range of products.

Today, Hildebrand Farms Dairy is a model of a successful, modern family dairy operation. They've managed to grow and adapt while staying true to their roots and maintaining the quality that has been their hallmark for generations.

As Mary reflected on their journey, she said with a mix of pride and humility, "We were fools, and we did it." But their "foolishness" has resulted in a thriving business that not only produces excellent dairy products but also preserves a way of life and educates the public about the importance of local agriculture.

Farm to Table: Hildebrand's Product Line

Hildebrand Farms Dairy offers a diverse range of products that showcase the quality of their milk. Their staples include whole milk, 2% milk, skim, creamline, and chocolate milk, but they don't stop there. They also produce strawberry milk and a unique root beer milk that Mary described as "think of a root beer float, but the ice cream is melted in."

One of their standout products is their cream-line milk. Mary explained its benefits:

"We have had several people come back to me, friends and strangers alike, and say, 'You know, I can't have dairy, but I can drink your creamline milk.'"

Their seasonal offerings include a much-anticipated eggnog available from October through early January. They've also ventured into ice cream production and hand-churn their own butter, a labor-intensive process that Mary estimated takes about 30 minutes per jar.

All of these products are bottled in glass, which not only keeps the milk cooler but also eliminates any plastic taste, and waste.

Community Engagement and Education

For the Hildebrands, running a dairy isn't just about producing milk—it's about educating the public and engaging with their community. They offer tours of their facility, allowing visitors to see the entire process from milking to bottling.

Their annual Fall Festival, held in October, is a customer appreciation event that draws thousands of visitors. "People come and stay the entire day, which just blows our mind," Mary says. The festival includes food trucks, live music, free tours, and activities for children.

They also participate in June Dairy Month with special events and promotions, and have even hosted yoga classes on the farm.

Looking to the Future

Despite their success, the Hildebrands aren't content to rest on their laurels. Mary dreams of expanding their educational offerings:

"One of our dreams, well, my dream, I'd love to have a venue or a place where people could rent out. And I have visions of having a kitchen area... do a cooking demonstration."

They're also considering venturing into cheese production, though Mary acknowledges the challenges: "That's a whole 'nother set of equipment and everything. And finding a cheese maker is difficult."

Whatever the future holds, the Hildebrands remain committed to their core values of quality, education, and family. They continue to innovate while honoring their Swiss-American roots.

From Arnold's bouquet of edelweiss to the glass bottles of milk on store shelves today, Hildebrand Farms Dairy embodies the American dream—a story of immigration, hard work, and family dedication. It's a place where visitors can not only taste some of the best dairy products Kansas has to offer but also connect with a rich agricultural heritage that continues to thrive in the heart of America.

So the next time you're in Junction City, stop by Hildebrand Farms Dairy. Pick up a bottle of cream-line milk and products from local makers, savor their homemade ice cream, or join a tour to learn about modern dairy farming. You'll be participating in a legacy nearly a century in the making—and tasting the difference that dedication makes.

Hildebrand Farms Dairy
5210 Rucker Rd
Junction City, KS 66441
(785)238-8029
hildebrandfarmsdairy.com

Rathert Field and Junction City Brigade

IF YOU WANT TO experience baseball as it was meant to be, visit Rathert Field in Junction City. This historic ballpark not only offers visitors a glimpse into the past, it also celebrates America's pastime of today.

Rathert Field is home base for the Junction City Brigade, a summer collegiate baseball team. Founded in 2012 with their first game in 2013, this team is no diamond in the rough. As of 2024, they've won the Mid-Plains League championship all but three years since the founding of the league a decade earlier.

Why is the JC Brigade such a winning team? When I asked General Manager Cecil Aska, he jokingly said, "Me," and then he turned serious. He attributes their record to the community's commitment to providing opportunities and to the local businesses. "There has been always a history of of some baseball flowing through this community," he said. He gestured to the signs hanging on the outfield fence. "We have great sponsors...the community support in terms of business, that's a real key to us being successful."

That community support stretches back to the very beginnings of this piece of Junction City's past.

History of Rathert Field

It was 1936, in the middle of the Great Depression, and Junction City wanted a baseball team. That meant they needed a field. Fortunately, FDR's Work Projects Administration (at the time known as Works Progress Administration) was helping communities like theirs all over the country. Junction City applied in September of the same year. On July 18, 1937, the "Jay Cees" played their first game in Rathert Field to a sold-out crowd of 1,400.

They named the field for city engineer Arthur Rathert because of the amount of effort he put into securing the project. Not your typical stadium, Rathert Field is made of limestone and has several innovative features. The stadium's architect incorporated tunnels under the stands and strategically placed windows to create natural air circulation, combating Kansas heat. Cecil said it's always about ten degrees cooler in the stands than anywhere else.

The Jay Cees joined the Ban Johnson league, the premier semi-pro league in the Midwest, and continued to play until 1941, when baseball was suspended due to World War II. However, that didn't mean the field was empty. Soldiers from Fort Riley would come to Rathert Field to play ball, often with locals who hadn't gone off to war. Although it's rumored that Jackie Robinson played at Rathert while he was stationed at Fort Riley, there's no definitive proof.

Baseball Hall of Fame inductee Buck O'Neil played at Rathert during his time with the Kansas City Monarchs, a member of the Negro leagues. More recently, MLB star Albert Pujols stepped up to the plate while he played for the Hays Larks.

According to the Black History Trail of Geary County, "Rathert Field was one of the places that welcomed the K. C. Monarchs to practice and play."

After the war, baseball resumed all over the country, including in Junction City, although the names and leagues changed. The Junction City Soldiers played in the 1950s, followed by the Hawks, the Merchants, and the Generals. Following the Generals' last game in 2010, baseball took a sideline for a couple years until six locals, including Cecil, formed the Junction City Community Baseball Club.

In 2013, the club founded the Junction City Brigade. The next year, the team became a founding member of the Mid-Plains League. They won that first championship and six more, including in 2024.

While Cecil joked that he was the reason for the team's success, his management style definitely fosters growth and independence. Both his players and his managers are college or university students, and they get real-world experience. Instead of Cecil recruiting players, he gives the managers that responsibility. "I operate on a philosophy of, okay, you're hired. Do your job." He said he keeps an eye on them and will reel them back in if they go too far off path. "I don't overly interfere," he said, "but trust me—I know what's going on... I give them that experience and learning how to take that manager role."

It seems to be working.

They also offer internships and work experiences for local youth, collaborating with universities like Kansas State. These internships cover various aspects of sports management, from marketing to game day operations.

Over the years, Rathert Field has undergone several renovations while maintaining its original charm. The original ticket booth still stands, and the dugouts maintain their below-field-level design. "This is how the dugout has always been," Cecil explained.

Recent improvements include turf installation in 2019 to address longstanding drainage issues. "We used to call this Lake Rathert," Cecil chuckled. "It would hold water, and you had to do a lot of rescheduling."

GameTime Athletics, located in a suburb of Kansas City, installed the turf along with some other improvements. Although they repair athletic fields all over the country, this is what they had to say about Rathert Field:

"It would be hard to beat a better example of a ball field in our minds, one that speaks to history, and one that gives you a warm and fuzzy feeling like that of the Rathert Stadium Ball Park in Junction City, KS."

> TLTip: While many people call it Rathert Stadium the official name is Rathert Field.

It's fitting that Cecil now heads up his hometown team. He grew up a literal baseball throw from Rathert Field: if a player hit a ball over the fence, it could end up in his backyard. He remembered when there was a wheat field between the stadium and the airport, and he and his friends would race the planes. He also mentioned the former rodeo grounds and sale barn that once stood nearby, painting a picture of how the area evolved.

"This is my field," he said.

Today, the JC Brigade draws about 6,000 fans over their two-month season, offering affordable family entertainment. Future renovations will include replacing the aging scoreboard and fence and updating the beer garden area. Any changes will keep the historic character of the field in mind.

With its rich history and community focus, Rathert Field and the Junction City Brigade offer more than just baseball games; they provide a link to the past, opportunities for the future, and a gathering place for the community. As you sit in the limestone stands, listening to the crack of the bat and feeling the breeze through those ingeniously designed windows, you're not just watching a game—you're experiencing a piece of living history.

Junction City Brigade
785-375-1483
jcbrigade.com
Rathert Field
900 W 13th St
Junction City, KS 66441

Historical Attractions

Overview

IN GEARY COUNTY, THE past is not only remembered, but actively preserved. The Geary County Historical Society safeguards the area's history, curating exhibits and collections that offer insight into the lives of early settlers through people and businesses of the 19th Century, Native American cultures, and the military's longstanding presence in the area. One of the key historical influences is Fort Riley, home to several museums that delve deep into the pivotal role the U.S. Army played in both local and national history. From the Custer House, which showcases frontier military life, to the U.S. Cavalry Museum, these sites offer a tangible connection to the past.

If you'd like to step into yesterday, these historical attractions will immerse you in the complex past of Geary County. You'll encounter stories of resilience and transformation, from Geary County's early settlement days through its involvement in shaping the American West, up to its modern military significance. Whether you're retracing the steps of 19th-century soldiers or uncovering local stories that left a national impact, these historical sites ensure that Geary County's vibrant past continues to educate and inspire.

Geary County Historical Society

Where Past Meets Present

IF YOU WANT TO get a better understanding of a place, visit its history museum. While it can be easy to walk into a place that preserves items from the past and picture them as dusty old relics, the truth is, those cases, exhibits, and dioramas protect not only a bunch of old stuff; they tell the stories of people, and they tell the stories of place.

As Geary County Historical Society Director and Curator Heather Hagedorn said, "We all become history, eventually."

Her comment was regarding her efforts to encourage locals to donate present-day items, but it articulated one reason history museums are such an important way to get to know a community.

Geary County Historical Society's story began in 1972 as an attempt to save an historic blacksmith shop. "A group of history-loving people got together and created the Historical Society," Heather said. They weren't able to save the building, but the society remained. They collected items, rented a building on 7th Street, and had a small museum. "We'll use the term loosely."

Eventually, they needed larger, more permanent digs. Fortunately, a space became available.

The Geary County Historical Society is in a building that is itself historic. Built in 1903, it was the high school until 1929, when the last senior class graduated. The high school may have moved, but the building remained a place for education. For the next four decades, it was a Departmental School for kindergartners and sixth graders.

In the 1970s, the three-story building held Head Start classes and special education programs, but by 1980, the structure was woefully out of date and it was vacated. It had fallen into such disrepair the city talked about tearing it down to put up apartment buildings.

Fortunately, the Geary County Historical Society needed a home. Even more fortunately, a local family got one for them. Fred and Dorothy Bramlage bought the building to save it, then donated it to the society. The couple were active philanthropists: the Dorothy Bramlage Public Library serves Junction City, and if you've seen a Kansas State basketball game in Manhattan, it was in the Fred Bramlage Coliseum.

It took about ten years to get the building up to standard, including adding elevators and more bathrooms. Much of the museum's interior was transformed to house exhibits instead of classrooms. However, one classroom still exists on the second floor, and you can see what it would have been like to attend as a student.

Today's museum comprises three floors of exhibits. They only have enough room to display about an eighth of their holdings, so some displays are rotated.

In the basement, you can see a print shop like the one that published the Daily Union, which can trace its beginnings to 1858. The first floor includes a "main street" exhibit that shows the types of shops residents in the late 19th and early 20th centuries would have patronized, including a blacksmith. There's also "grandma's kitchen." It illustrates the effort involved in ironing, doing the laundry, and other day-to-day chores, and it's enough to make you appreciate modern conveniences. There are also indigenous artifacts and remnants from a mastodon.

Also on the first floor are several photographs of early prominent Junction City residents. These date back to the 1920s and were from the first effort to create a historical society. Unfortunately, at that time, women were referred to only by their husband's name.

Because of dedicated research, all but two of the women now have the dignity of their own.

The second floor is where you'll find that classroom, and there's an auditorium where they host themed events like their popular murder mysteries. That's also where you'll learn about local businesses, including Stacy's Restaurant. This Grandview Plaza spot opened in 1954 and is still serving comfort food today. And don't miss the Ferris Wheel of Shoes. W.H. Moses designed a display in the shape of a Ferris wheel for his dry goods store, and Heather was so inspired she asked a local to replicate it.

In addition to the old high school, the Geary County Historical Society has been collecting other structures. Adjacent to the museum stands the Starcke House, once owned by a prominent jeweler family. This Victorian-era home not only showcases period architecture and furnishings but also holds intriguing family stories that continue to unfold as new information comes to light.

On the west side of town, the Society maintains the Spring Valley Historic Site. On its grounds is a one-room schoolhouse that operated from 1873 to 1958. Remarkably, this school never had running water or electricity throughout its 85 years of operation. "We have a board member who went to school there," Heather noted, providing a direct link to this piece of educational history.

The same site also houses two relocated log cabins. One of these, the Wetzel Cabin, holds particular significance as the location of the first Lutheran congregation west of the Mississippi.

The Society's last acquisition was St. Joseph's Church, which they purchased in 2008. Listed on the State Register of Historic Place, it's a work in progress. Improvements have included a new roof, front doors, some windows, and electricity and light fixtures.

Heather described it as "definitely a grassroots effort from the community out there who just really believe in that project." This restoration underscores the Society's dedication to preserving not just artifacts, but entire structures that hold historical and cultural significance for the community.

One of the Society's most innovative initiatives focuses on collecting oral histories from community members. "We do a Memories at the Museum program," Heather explained, "which is all about collecting oral histories, and letting people tell their stories while they're alive rather than waiting and making it harder for historians in the future."

This program has captured invaluable firsthand accounts of significant historical periods and experiences, including stories from World War II veterans and accounts of growing up Black in Junction City during the 1960s and 1970s.

The Society has also collaborated with the Black History Trail project. "We've partnered with them to help them tell the stories through the trail," Heather said. The Society is creating the signs for the trail and plans eventually to have an exhibit with artifacts. *See the Black History Trail chapter for more information.*

Through exhibits, oral histories, and preservation efforts, the Geary County Historical Society tells the story of the community. Whether you're a history buff or just curious about Junction City's roots, this museum provides a unique and engaging look into how the past shapes its present, and perhaps offer insight into its future.

Geary County Historical Society
530 N Adams, Junction City, KS 66441 (785)238-1666
gearyhistory.org

THERESA L. GOODRICH

Spring Valley Historic Site
K-18 and Spring Valley Road

St. Joseph's Historic Church
13497 Lower McDowell Creek Road

C.L. Hoover Opera House

THE C.L. HOOVER OPERA House is one of Junction City's finest attractions. With its soaring clock tower and stunning red-bricked face, it stands out and is a fitting home for the area's cultural organizations. This landmark began as a public hall and is now a complex containing every Geary County arts agency: the Junction

City Little Theater, Junction City Arts Council, and Junction City Community Band.

Like many historic buildings, it's gone through several changes in its long life.

The story of C.L. Opera House begins on July 15, 1880, when the citizens of Junction City voted to pay $12,000 to build a public hall. In today's figures, that would be like voluntarily paying a third of a million dollars and, at the time, the population was only around 2,700. By January 1882, they had their public hall, a Romanesque-style building in red brick with a Geary County limestone foundation.

This hall served multiple purposes: the front housed the jail, the police department, and the fire station. The fire department's horses lived in stalls in the basement. The city council room occupied the second floor. In the back portion of the building was the opera house. Originally planned for a capacity of 1,000, they could only install 600 seats because of budgeting issues.

It wasn't long before they remodeled the interior, and when they unveiled the new hall on January 1, 1890, they christened it the Blakely Opera House after a prominent resident who'd passed away five years prior.

Sadly, in 1898, a roaring fire ripped through the building. It was almost a total loss; only the front exterior wall remained. There was some question about whether they should rebuild, but within eight months, Junction City had an opera house again.

They kept the original red brick and built the entire back portion of the building with native limestone. They erected a whole new clock tower, this time complete with a 2,500-pound bell. An article about the fire in the Junction City Weekly Union from January 21, 1898, hoped for a building that would last twenty years. In 1919, they reconfigured the hall to welcome both live theater and those new-fangled motion pictures.

During this time, the building still housed city offices, but in 1937, the city got its own building and moved out. Five years later, the Opera House transformed once again, this time into a modern movie theater with air conditioning. With blocked-in windows and a painted white exterior, the new Colonial Theater screened movies until 1982.

While the building was in danger of being lost after the theater closed, local philanthropists Fred and Dorothy Bramlage purchased the structure and donated it to the city. In 2003, the Opera House received a State Historic Register designation, and renovation finally began in 2007. Seven million dollars later, it re-opened to the public the next year.

That renovation, led by city manager Rod Barnes, was a significant undertaking. While it brought the building up to modern standards, it also presented some challenges. For instance, they placed the director's office upstairs, disconnecting it from the day-to-day activities, and they'd stuck the kitchen in an impractical location.

Since the renovation, the opera house has seen further improvements. Joe and Sheila Markley, former music teachers, took over management in 2014. They're retiring at the end of 2024, but during their ten-year tenure, they definitely made their mark, working to address the quirks of the 2008 renovation and expand the building's use.

One notable addition has been the contributions of local craftsman John York. York, whose grandfather and uncle helped build the city's municipal building, has created and donated numerous pieces of furniture and art to the opera house. His work evokes Frank Lloyd Wright and includes custom mirrors, tables, and chairs. He even installed stained glass windows in the doors of a storage closet, which the Markleys dubbed "The Chapel."

The Markleys also oversaw the expansion of community programs. The opera house now hosts a variety of events, from theatrical performances to educational workshops. They've created multi-use spaces, including rehearsal halls and meeting rooms, and made practical improvements like adding sinks to various rooms.

In recent years, the clock tower has undergone another restoration. A $25,000 project, partly funded by a generous donation from a Manhattan resident, brought the bell back to working order. The dedication ceremony featured a creative touch, with attendees given pinwheels to celebrate the moment.

Today, the C.L. Hoover Opera House is the centerpiece of Junction City's arts community. It hosts national acts and is home to the community theater, arts council, and an expanding youth program. The building now includes art galleries and display spaces, showcasing local talent.

The C.L. Hoover Opera House stands as a testament to Junction City's commitment to the arts. From its beginnings as a multi-purpose public hall to its current status as a cultural hub, it has weathered fires, transformations, and the changing tides of entertainment. Through it all, it has remained a central part of Junction City's identity, continuing to adapt while honoring its storied past.

C.L. Hoover Opera House
135 W 7th St Junction City, KS 66441 785-238-3906
jcoperahouse.org

Heritage Park

HERITAGE PARK IS A public square filled with monuments that celebrate the community and pay tribute to its military past. Since 1958, this park has been a part of Junction City.

When the town was originally platted, the founders left a block open at the corner of 6th and Washington to be used as a city park. Because it was an open square, some early residents decided they could lay claim to the land. In the mid- and late-1860s, the city had to evict squatters who'd erected houses, fences, and cattle pens, seemingly overnight.

For 130 years, the space was known simply as City Park or Uptown Park. Over the years, the city built monument after monument honoring its past. Then in 1988, local resident Geri Hoffman suggested Heritage Park, winning a city-wide essay contest, and it became official.

The most recognizable symbol of Junction City is the Grand Army of the Republic (GAR) Monument, an impressive stone arch that commands attention. Erected in 1898, it was the first monument constructed in the park. It's 35-feet-tall, made of native stone, and honors the soldiers of the Civil War. At the top, a soldier stands tall and is flanked by two cannons. Those cannons replaced civil war bayonets, which had been repeatedly blown down by the strong Kansas winds.

At the center of the block is the Heritage Park Fountain, a legacy of one of the first graduates of the Junction City High School building on Adams, which is now home to the Geary County Historical Society. Jacob Benton Callen was active in local government from 1880 to 1937, and when he died in 1937, he bequeathed $3,000 "for the specific purpose of purchasing and installing an electrically lighted fountain in the park."

There's also a bandstand, which is actually in its third incarnation. The first bandstand was built in 1878 entirely of wood, and the second in 1911. It lasted until 1973, but the current bandstand wasn't built until 1996. The JCHS class of 1946 helped to raise the money for the new structure, making this a true community project. They dedicated the bandstand to veterans, inspired by a local's memories of WWII soldiers meeting their sweethearts in the park.

The American War Mothers dedicated the World War I Monument, a stone planter, in 1928. It pays tribute to soldiers lost in the Great War. In 2016, Lincoln Elementary School students raised funds to restore this monument.

The Kansas Vietnam War Memorial, constructed in 1985, was the first and only Vietnam memorial in Kansas at the time of its construction. Because of that, it became the official state memorial in 1991. It lists the names of 753 Kansans who died in the war and 38 who were missing at the time of dedication. It also displays the Vietnam War Campaign and Purple Heart medals. The Purple Heart Monument was unveiled in 2010 to celebrate the 50th anniversary of the founding of the Military Order of the Purple Heart. Members of this order, MOPH for short, have received the Purple Heart Medal for wounds suffered in combat.

Other notable monuments include the Law Enforcement Monument (2007), and the POW/MIA, KIA/WIA Monument (2014).

The park also features several commemorative trees, including an Eisenhower Green Ash planted in 2000 to honor a local veteran, and a Maple tree dedicated in 1985 to those who fought or went missing in the Vietnam and Korean Wars.

The Bicentennial Time Capsule will give future residents and visitors of Junction City a glimpse into the past. Buried in 1976 to celebrate the United States' Bicentennial, it contains about 350 items and 250 personal messages from that era and will be opened a hundred years later, in 2076. This snapshot of Junction City will unveil into the city's history.

Heritage Park offers a unique opportunity to explore Junction City's rich history through its monuments. Each tells a story of service, sacrifice, and community spirit that has shaped the city over the years.

Corner of 6th and Washington, Junction City, KS 66441

Fort Riley

Since 1853, Fort Riley has been a key part of American military history. This base in the Flint Hills has changed with the needs of the U.S. Army and a growing nation.

The fort began as a frontier outpost and a base to provide military escorts to settlers moving west, but soldiers based at Fort Riley quickly took on the role of peacekeepers as tensions escalated over slavery. During the ensuing Civil War, Fort Riley became, as Fort Riley Museum Complex Director Emeritus Robert J. Smith,

Ph.D. called it, "a backwater." Regular units left to join the fighting and militia units stayed to protect caravans still heading west. Despite being far from the main action, Fort Riley still played a role and was a POW camp for confederate soldiers.

After the war, Fort Riley's protection extended to the new railroad lines crossing the nation, and in 1866, the 7th Cavalry Regiment mustered-in. That winter, Brevet Maj. Gen. George A. Custer took charge of that regiment. Though Custer's time at Fort Riley was short - only about 6-8 months - it left a lasting mark on the fort's history.

In the 1870s, there was talk of closing Fort Riley. The frontier was moving further west, and the Army questioned the need for the post. In the 1880s, General Phil Sheridan saw potential in Fort Riley. According to Dr. Smith, Sheridan liked two things: the vast grasslands for feeding cavalry horses, and the railroad for easy transport. Sheridan also wanted to improve the cavalry after its underwhelming performance in the Civil War.

His solution? A cavalry school, which lasted from the mid-1880s until just after the end of World War II. The last tactical horse unit became inactive in March 1947.

Famous figures like George Patton and Hap Arnold spent time at Fort Riley during this period. Patton had been there three times: as a student, an instructor, and a director of the Cavalry School.

Fort Riley also played a significant role in the history of the Buffalo Soldiers. The 9th and 10th Cavalry Regiments, comprised of African American soldiers, were stationed at Fort Riley at various times. These units, nicknamed 'Buffalo Soldiers' by Native Americans, served with distinction on the frontier, in the Spanish-American War, in the Philippines, while monitoring the

Mexican border during World War I, and in the European Theater in World War II. Their story is told at the Buffalo Soldier Memorial in Junction City.

World War I brought big changes to Fort Riley. In 1917, the Army built Camp Funston on the east side of the main post. Dr. Smith said it was practically built overnight. It trained over 50,000 soldiers for World War 1.

Camp Funston had a unique concept. Dr. Smith explained that "it was kind of an open air mall. It had shops. It had the world's largest barbershop. I think it had like 64 chairs." The idea was to keep soldiers on post while giving them amenities and a place for families to visit.

Between the wars, Fort Riley kept busy with cavalry training. In the 1920s, future Air Force leader Hap Arnold practiced coordinating ground troops with aircraft there.

When World War II hit, Fort Riley had become a major training center again. About 150,000 soldiers trained before heading to battlefields in Europe and the Pacific.

In 1955, Fort Riley became the home of the 1st Infantry Division. Dr. Smith noted, "The 1st Infantry Division is the oldest continuously serving division in the army, established in 1917, and it's still around today. Never been broken up."

Since then, Fort Riley has been involved in nearly every major U.S. conflict. The 1st Infantry Division spent almost five years in Vietnam. Later, it took part in operations in Kuwait, the Balkans, Iraq, and Afghanistan.

Fort Riley continued its role in global operations, including NATO missions and security operations in Eastern Europe.

Throughout its history, Fort Riley has shown remarkable adaptability. As Dr. Smith said, "Fort Riley has always been able to adjust to the Army's mission."

Fort Riley evolved from a frontier outpost to a cavalry training center, and then to a modern military installation. Its ability to change with the times has kept it relevant and crucial to the U.S. Army. From "Bleeding Kansas" to global operations, it's been a key player in the nation's military efforts.

Museums and Historical Attractions at Fort Riley

Fort Riley is a piece of living history, with monuments and museums celebrating its rich heritage. Admission to the museums is free and each gives a different insight into the past. Please confirm hours of operation. See the Visiting Fort Riley FAQs chapter for details on access to the base.

For a great overview of the fort and the significant structures, there are both self-guided driving and walking tours. Visit fortril eyhistoricalsociety.org for printable PDFs of both.

United States Cavalry Museum

Located in Fort Riley's original hospital, which was built in 1855, the United States Cavalry Museum showcases the history of the mounted horse soldier from the Revolutionary War to the cavalry's final inactivations in 1950. Exhibits include cavalry uniforms, weapons, and artifacts, along with information about the cavalry's role in American military history, from the frontier days to World War II.

First Infantry Division Museum

Dedicated to the storied history of the 1st Infantry Division, also known as "Big Red One," this museum covers the division's involvement in major U.S. conflicts, from World War I to present-day operations. The museum features immersive exhibits, personal stories from soldiers, and displays of equipment used by the division. It's located in a 1905 building that was originally constructed as barracks for the Cavalry School Band.

Custer House

Open Memorial Day through Labor Day

This historic home, named after General George Armstrong Custer, is a restored 19th-century residence that provides a glimpse into frontier military life. Built in 1855, the building is the only remaining set of officers' quarters from the fort's inception. Today, furnishings represent the late 1870s and early 1880s, the period when Custer was stationed at Fort Riley.

First Territorial Capitol of Kansas

Open mid-April to mid-October

Operated by the Kansas Historical Society, this museum is housed in the original building where Kansas' first territorial legislature met in 1855. It provides insights into the political struggles of the "Bleeding Kansas" era, as well as Kansas' journey to statehood.

Fort Riley Post Cemetery

Established in 1853, the Post Cemetery is one of the oldest historic properties at the fort. Three Medal of Honor recipients are buried on its grounds, indicated by a gold star on their tombstones. There are also confederate graves as well as German and Italian prisoners of war.

Atomic Annie

SOUTH OF I-70 AND the Henry Gate entrance to Fort Riley is a piece of Cold War history. In the 1950s, the United States built massive 85-ton cannons that could fire atomic weapons. Known as Atomic Annie, the military only produced twenty and only three remain. Although the cannons, officially named M65, were deployed to Europe and Korea, they had a short service life and were decommissioned in 1963.

You can see one of these cannons in Freedom Park. A winding gravel path leads you from the parking lot to the 84-foot-long weapon. Along the way are World War II-era howitzers and other military equipment. Once you reach the top of the hill, you're treated to a commanding view of Fort Riley. The path to the stop can be steep in some places, so be sure to wear appropriate shoes.

Freedom Park also recognizes another piece of American history that goes back even further in time. In the mid-1800s, Mormons crossed this area to escape persecution. An historical marker tells the story of this South Fork of the Mormon Trail. In addition to Mormons, the military, settlers, and freighters also used the trail.

Freedom Park/Atomic Annie
Interstate 70, Exit 301

Black History Trail

THE BLACK HISTORY TRAIL of Geary County highlights the history and culture of African Americans in Junction City, Fort Riley, and beyond. Established in 2021, this self-guided tour provides insights into the contributions and struggles of African Americans in Geary County, from the Buffalo Soldiers to community leaders. It's a valuable resource for both visitors and residents interested in local history.

Founded in November 2021, the origins of the trail can be traced back to the late 1990s and early 2000s. Jim Sands, a retired Army Sergeant Major, was inspired by two Buffalo Soldiers, Albert Curley and Nolan Self, who asked him to preserve their legacy. Part of that legacy had been honored with the erection of the Buffalo Soldier Memorial in October 2000. Curley was instrumental in its construction, and he and four other surviving Buffalo Soldiers were present at the dedication.

The Buffalo Soldiers were members of the 9th and 10th Cavalry Regiments, two of six black regiments created after the Civil War. The 10th was founded in Fort Leavenworth, and both regiments were stationed at Fort Riley at various times. The Buffalo Soldier Memorial is in Pawnee Park, next to the red brick houses that had been segregated housing for the soldiers and their families.

Both the Buffalo Soldier Memorial and Pawnee Park are stops on the Black History Trail.

Another important stop is the VFW Post 8773. This post began in 1946 after the existing VFW - Veterans of Foreign Wars - turned away a group of men. These men had fought in World War II, a war on foreign soils. They were veterans. Yet they were turned away because they were black.

Instead of letting that slide, the soldiers created their own. VFW Post 8773 is still active, serves the community, and is open to everyone.

Other sites include historic Rathert Field, completed in 1937. Made of native limestone, it's been described as "the finest baseball stadium in Kansas." Negro League baseball stars "Buck" O'Neil and Satchel Page played there, and today it's home to the Junction City Brigade.

Highland Cemetery, which was at one time the only place Black people could be buried, and Second Missionary Baptist Church are also poignant. The church began in 1873 and was originally known as the First Colored Baptist Church.

The Geary County Historical Society has partnered with the Black History Trail to research and write the informational signs displayed at the various stops. As of 2024, adding these markers is an ongoing project.

Visit blackhistorytrailofgearycounty.org for more information.

The Great Outdoors

Overview

GEARY COUNTY IS KNOWN for its beautiful Great Outdoors. Situated in the heart of the Flint Hills, it's a place of wide open skies with endless opportunities for adventure.

Milford Lake is the star attraction. As the largest lake in the state, this reservoir draws fishing enthusiasts from across the country. It's surrounded by parks, including Milford State Park and several areas managed by the Army Corps of Engineers, where you can hike, horseback ride, camp, or hit the trails on an ATV. While you're there, don't miss the Milford Nature Center and Fish Hatchery—especially the charming butterfly enclosure.

Geary State Fishing Lake and Wildlife Area offers another out-door retreat and is great for birdwatching. A popular fishing spot, this manmade lake is stocked with bass, catfish, and more. There are also trails within Junction City. Golf enthusiasts can enjoy a round at Rolling Meadows Golf Course, an 18-hole public course featuring beautiful views of the surrounding countryside.

Are you ready to get outside and explore beautiful Geary county?

Milford State Park

MILFORD STATE PARK IS a haven for outdoor enthusiasts and nature lovers alike. This park offers a smorgasbord of activities for nature lovers, water enthusiasts, and campers. It's the kind of place where you can pitch a tent under the stars, reel in a whopper of a fish, or simply kick back and watch the sunset paint the sky.

Whether you're planning a family vacation, a fishing trip with friends, or a solo escape into nature, Milford State Park's got it.

Camping & Lodging

Whether you're a seasoned outdoors enthusiast or prefer a touch of comfort, Milford accommodates all styles. Choose from over eight campgrounds with over 250 campsites. Several have electric and water hookups, ideal for RVers who crave a comfortable camping experience. Tent campers can opt for primitive sites. There's a separate campground for equestrians.

For those seeking a roof over their heads, cabins are available. While not luxury accommodations, they provide beds, air conditioning, and stunning lake views. Linens are not included, so pack accordingly.

Watersports and Fishing

Milford Reservoir is a haven for anglers. Dubbed the "Fishing Capital of Kansas," the lake teems with walleye, crappie, catfish, and bass. Don't have a boat? No worries. Cast a line from the shore. There are multiple fish cleaning stations. There's also an ADA Fishing Dock with kayak launch.

If you want to get out on the water, you can rent a boat from the full-service marina. Stock up on your fishing and boating needs at On the Docks Convenience Store.

On scorching summer days, cool off at the splash park or with a refreshing dip in the lake from the sand beach.

Trails and Wildlife

There are several trails at Milford State Park. The longest, at 6.1 miles, is Eagle Ridge Trail. Two of the trails are open for hikers and mountain bikers, and the others are also open to equestrians.

Be on the lookout for wildlife, including deer, wild turkeys, and a variety of other birds. In the winter, the lake is home to several bald eagles.

Essential Information

- **Entrance Fees:** A daily vehicle permit costs $5 (as of 2024) or opt for an annual pass for $25.

- **Reservations:** Securing campsites and cabins in advance is recommended, especially during peak season (May to September).

- **Pet Policy:** Leashed pets are welcome.

- **Responsible Recreation:** Alcohol is allowed, but please drink responsibly.

Milford State Park

3612 State Park Road, Milford, KS 66514 785-238-3014
ksoutdoors.com/State-Parks/Locations/Milford

Milford Nature Center and Fish Hatchery

MILFORD NATURE CENTER OFFERS a fascinating glimpse into Kansas wildlife. Whether you're a budding naturalist or just looking to spend an afternoon learning about local flora and fauna, this facility will captivate curious minds of all ages.

The center features both indoor and outdoor exhibits. Outside, you'll find several raptors that, unable to survive in the wild, now call the center home. There's also a clever birdwatching wall with peepholes, allowing visitors to observe birds in their natural habitat without disturbing them.

Kids (and the young at heart) can enjoy a fun maze and playground. These offer both an entertaining challenge and a chance to burn off some energy between exhibits.

Inside the main building, dioramas created by renowned artist Terry Chase of Chase Studio showcase Kansas habitats. Interactive displays and informative panels provide hands-on learning about the Sunflower State's ecology.

The live animal room is a highlight, housing native Kansas creatures from snakes to a dollhouse filled with cockroaches. The star resident is the black-footed ferret, one of North America's rarest mammals and once thought extinct.

During warmer months, a colorful butterfly garden buzzes with activity, educating visitors about the crucial role of pollinators in our ecosystem.

Short nature trails around the center offer a chance to stretch your legs and apply what you've learned.

Behind the center, you'll find the Milford Fish Hatchery, one of only six warm water hatcheries in the USA. It's a major contributor to Kansas's excellent fishing, stocking lakes across the state. You can walk around the "raceways" where fish are raised, though they might be hard to spot in the murky (but clean) lake or well water. While most are bottom feeders, you might catch a glimpse of colorful koi.

The center hosts various programs and events throughout the year, from guided hikes to educational workshops. Check their calendar before visiting to see what's happening.

Best of all, admission to the Milford Nature Center is free!

Milford Nature Center
3415 Hatchery Dr, Junction City, KS 66441 785-238-5323
ksoutdoors.com

Spotlight on Konza Prairie

I AWOKE EARLY MY last morning in Geary County. I wanted to see the sun rise over the Flint Hills. It crested the horizon as I drove east, bursting in bright orange, forcing me to squint as I tried to keep my eyes on the road.

Tried, but didn't always succeed.

One thing I've heard locals boast of in my several visits to Kansas is the immensity of the sky, its beauty. It's not the only state to claim that—Montana is Big Sky Country, after all—but that doesn't diminish their statement.

It *is* big. It *is* beautiful. It is commanding.

It takes your breath away.

So, too, did my hike in Konza Prairie Biological Station. Anyone who says Kansas is flat hasn't gotten off the interstate. Sure, there aren't mountains, but the earth undulates, occasionally halting in bluffs and cliffs.

As my thighs can attest, Konza Prairie is most certainly *not* flat.

Dew still dripped from the tall grasses when I arrived. At first, the trail was easy. I crossed a short suspension bridge over a shallow creek, walking through stands of oaks and hackberry. It quickly led to prairie, but the land was still in shadow because the sun hadn't quite crested the hill in the distance. It felt like walking in Las Vegas: that giant casino looks like it's close, but that's only because you don't realize how big it is until you've walked half a mile and you're still not there.

For a microsecond, I looked at that giant hill and thought about turning around.

Even though there were a few cars in the gravel parking lot when I'd arrived, I hadn't seen anyone. It was just the grasshoppers, the birds, the butterflies, and me. They were in their element.

So was I, although you couldn't tell as my breathing became increasingly more labored the higher I went. I knew, though, I just knew that if I kept pushing, if I kept going, I'd be rewarded. As an overweight woman in her fifties who's a recent cancer survivor and even more recently diagnosed diabetic, I know not to push myself too hard. I stopped when I needed to, drank plenty of water. Each time I did, I'd gaze around me in wonder. In the distance, a farmhouse shone in the morning sun. The shadows retreated, inch by inch, as I moved west, foot by foot.

The incline increased and the path changed from gravel to uneven stairs made of limestone. I picked my steps carefully, aware that a twisted ankle would be a huge problem. It wasn't even seven in the morning, I was in Kansas alone, and I still hadn't seen anyone on the trail. But I kept climbing, putting my hands on one thigh at a time, pushing to help my legs lift me up and up and up.

I reached the top. Aching, slightly, winded, and happy.

Oh, so very happy.

I turned slowly, getting a 360-degree view of the surrounding landscape, of the prairies, the hills, the undulating earth. The grasses swayed, the grasshoppers sang. When I faced the direction from which I'd come, I smiled ruefully. A strong, slender woman was running–running!–up the trail that had just kicked my butt. We nodded as she passed me, then turned left and ran towards the radio tower.

My breathing was louder than hers.

I still smiled. To be able to do that, to run up a tall hill in the early morning as the sun first blankets the land, what an incredible feeling that must be.

I took my time at the top of that hill. Not because I was tired, but because it was my last morning in Kansas and I wanted to soak it in. I understood why, over the years, Kansan after Kansan has told me that even though they couldn't wait to get away when they were growing up, they couldn't wait to get back after they'd realized what they'd left.

There was an information sign, so I read it. I heard voices and saw a trio walking up the trail. I passed them on my way down and we exchanged the normal pleasantries, as you do when hiking.

"Beautiful morning, isn't it?"

"Sure is."

I continued, soon passing another trio, this one a photographer and two young women. What a perfect place for a photo shoot, I thought. By the time I reached the end of the trail, I'd seen more people. The dew had dried in all but the shortest grasses. I got in my car and sipped my coffee, still warm despite my extended absence.

And as I drove back to Junction City to finish packing, to check out, and to begin my trek back home to Illinois, I saw the rising sun in my rearview mirror and smiled.

Hiking in Konza Prairie

Konza Prairie Nature Trail System is open for hiking from dawn to dusk every day. There are three trails:

- **Nature Trail Loop**: 2.6 miles

- **Kings Creek Loop**: 4.6 miles

- **Godwin Hill Loop**: 6.2 miles

Each trail offers opportunities to explore the diverse landscape, featuring lowland gallery forests, limestone ledges, and upland tallgrass prairie, with stunning views of the Flint Hills and the Kansas River Valley.

The trails are of moderate difficulty with occasional steep climbs and uneven terrain. The vast majority of KPBS is off-limits due to prairie conservation and research, so be sure to stay on the trail.

Note that pets, bicycles, drones, and horses are prohibited.

About Konza Prairie Biological Station

The Konza Prairie Biological Station (KPBS) is more than just a beautiful hiking destination. It's a 3,487-hectare (8,616-acre) native tallgrass prairie preserve and research station located in the Flint Hills of northeastern Kansas.

This unique outdoor laboratory is jointly owned by The Nature Conservancy and Kansas State University. KPBS serves as a field research station for the KSU Division of Biology.

The Konza Prairie Biological Station plays a crucial role in understanding and preserving the tallgrass prairie ecosystem.

Through its environmental research, KPBS contributes valuable data on how grasslands respond to environmental changes, informing conservation efforts and ecological predictions for similar ecosystems worldwide.

The station's work underscores the importance of preserving these vanishing landscapes, not just for their beauty, but for their ecological significance and the insights they provide into our changing world.

Konza Prairie Biological Station
McDowell Creek Rd, Manhattan, KS 66502 (785) 587-0441
keep.konza.k-state.edu

Geary State Fishing Lake and Wildlife Area

GEARY STATE FISHING LAKE is a 97-acre man-made lake, surrounded by 180 acres of public land, offering a more intimate outdoor experience compared to its larger cousin, Milford Reservoir.

Constructed in 1959, this compact lake packs a punch when it comes to fishing and wildlife viewing.

True to its name, Geary State Fishing Lake is a angler's paradise. The lake is stocked with a variety of fish species. It also offers excellent hunting opportunities. Birdwatchers will find plenty to observe, with a variety of waterfowl and other bird species frequenting the area.

While facilities are more primitive compared to larger state parks, Geary State Fishing Lake offers a small campground for those who want to extend their stay. Bring your own water and be prepared for a more rustic experience.

There are also picnic areas available, perfect for a lakeside lunch. Hiking trails wind through the area, offering opportunities to explore the diverse habitats surrounding the lake.

TLTip: Take a walk along the top of the dam to discover a charming waterfall near the spillway.

Geary State Fishing Lake and Wildlife Area
10 miles south of Junction City on K-57, KS 785-461-5402
ksoutdoors.com

Hunting & Fishing

HOME TO MILFORD RESERVOIR and the Milford Wildlife Area, Geary County is a hunting and fishing paradise. It's known as the fishing capital of Kansas and provides easy access to one of the largest blocks of public hunting lands in the state.

Fort Riley

It might surprise you, but you can hunt on Fort Riley. The base is known for being a great spot to hunt quail and elk, and also has turkeys, deer, pheasants, and greater prairie chickens. You'll need a special permit, but once that's granted, you can hunt on base on days when there are no Army exercises.

There are two permits: One is the Fort Riley Conservation Permit, which allows recreationists to "participate in all game hunting and non-hunting activities open on a given day. The other is the Outdoor Recreation Permit, which provides permission for fishing, hiking, shed antler hunting, or mushroom foraging. You can get information and apply for both at riley.isportsman.net.

Geary State Fishing Lake and Wildlife Area

Ten miles south of Junction City, Geary State Fishing Lake is surrounded by 180 acres of public hunting land. This man-made lake was constructed in 1959 and is stocked with largemouth bass, smallmouth bass, channel catfish, and more. For hunters, quail, squirrels, and rabbits are plentiful.

Milford Lake

Milford Lake is the largest man-made reservoir in the state, covering over 16,000 acres. This expansive body of water, combined with the surrounding wildlife area, offers a wealth of outdoor recreational opportunities for anglers, hunters, and nature enthusiasts alike. Milford Reservoir and Wildlife Area is managed by the U.S. Army Corps of Engineers.

Milford Lake is renowned for its excellent fishing. Anglers can expect to find an abundance of species including, walleye, crappie, white bass, largemouth bass, smallmouth bass, channel catfish, blue catfish, and flathead catfish. The lake hosts several fishing tournaments throughout the year, attracting anglers from across the region.

The Milford Wildlife Area encompasses over 19,000 acres of land surrounding the reservoir, providing ample opportunities for hunters. Game includes whitetail deer, turkey, quail, pheasant, waterfowl, rabbit and squirrel. It's one of the largest public hunting grounds in Kansas.

On the north side of the lake is the Steve Lloyd Refuge Area, which contains eight wetlands areas. Also open for hunting, this area adds another 1100 acres.

This area is also a great spot for birdwatching, boating, hiking, and camping.

Visit ksoutdoors.com for information on both Geary State Fishing Lake and Wildlife Area and Milford Reservoir and Wildlife Area.

Milford Wildlife Area
PO Box 301, Wakefield, KS 67487 785-461-5402

Sportsmen's Acres

Run by the Geary County Fish and Game Association, visit this shooting range to brush up on your skills. There's a pistol and rifle range, archery, and a trap range with voice calls. they also host multiple events and provide education.
K244 Spur, PO Box 631, Junction City, KS 66441 785-238-8727

More Outdoors

LOOKING FOR EVEN MORE ways to get outside? Geary County is home to several opportunities for al fresco adventures.

Golf

Rolling Meadows Golf Course is an 18-hole course designed by Richard Watson. The public course has six lakes and twenty-nine sand bunkers and has been highly rated by Golf Digest.

Rolling Meadows Golf Course
6514 Old Milford Rd, Milford, KS 66514 785-238-4303
jcrollingmeadows.com

Hiking and Biking

In addition to the trails at Milford State Park, Milford Nature Center, and Geary State Fishing Lake, there are other places for hiking and biking. Junction City has several trails, ranging from the short three-tenths of a mile circle around Bramlage Park to the Blue Jay Trail, which offers a connection to the high school. The Riverwalk Trail is a 4.8 mile gravel path along the Republican River between Fort Riley and the Milford Lake Outlet Tubes. From there, it becomes Old River Bluff trail at the Corp of Engineers Outlet park. If you want to keep going, the trail connects to those in Milford State Park.

There are also several trails within Fort Riley. Check that chapter for information on visiting the base.

Acorns Resort offers trails. You'll want to check in at the resort office first.

Additional hiking can be found at Konza Prairie Biological Station, Kansas Landscape Arboretum (Milford Lake), and Outlet Park (Milford Lake).

School Creek Park, on the west side of Milford Lake, has 287 acres of trails for Off-Road Vehicles. These ORVs must be 50 inches wide or less.

Dining in Geary County

Dining in Geary County

You won't go hungry in Geary County

ONE OF THE MOST surprising things about Geary County is the variety in its dining scene. Because the county is smaller, you might expect limited options. However, because the population is diverse, so is the cuisine. It also helps that Junction City has such a strong entrepreneurial bent. That's why there are several food trucks. For many restaurateurs, starting with a mobile business is a stepping stone.

Whether you want Italian, sushi, barbecue, Indian, or even Hawaiian, you'll find it in Geary County.

Below is a "taste" of what you can expect. Visit visitgearycounty. com for complete restaurant listings.

Bella's Italian Restaurant

Bella's Italian Restaurant is a great spot for a date night or an outing with friends and family. The stuffed mushrooms, filled with crabmeat and covered in Alfredo sauce, are a standout, and you can't go wrong with the pasta primavera. Service is attentive and friendly, portions are big, and prices are reasonable. They also offer brick-fired pizza, calzones, and a selection of Italian desserts.

605 Washington St. Junction City, KS 66441 785-762-1772
bellasitalianrestaurant.com

Blū Restaurant & Bar

Opened in December 2023 in a distinctive building across from Heritage Park, Blū Restaurant & Bar is a versatile addition to the Junction City dining scene. The menu is geared towards American cuisine and offers items like grilled salmon and chicken, Angus burgers, and a 16oz ribeye steak. The beef is procured from Munson Angus Farms, a family business dating back over 150 years.

The exposed-brick interior is tastefully decorated and includes homages to Kansas and the military. Blū is a family-friendly restaurant that's also a great choice for a date night.

602 N Washington St, Junction City, KS 785-390-0017

The Cove Bar & Grill

If you're looking for a great way to cap off a day on Milford Lake or just want the best sunset view in town, head to Acorns Resort and The Cove Bar & Grill. This lakeside spot is open year-round, and with live music, karaoke, game nights, and more, it's a great place to kick back and relax. Top picks from their menu include the Spicy Cajun Fried Boudin Balls, MB's Brisket Grilled Cheese, and Bonfire Shrimp Tacos.

3710 Farnum Creek Rd Milford, KS 66514 785-463-4000
acornsresortkansas.com

Crunch Bear

Crunch Bear is a small Japanese restaurant with limited seating. Menu items include dumplings, tempura, poke bowls, and sushi. Their "Chicken on a Stick" is crave-worthy delicious. They've also got a small gift shop if you want to pick up some souvenirs from your visit.

934 W Sixth Street, JC 785-492-4180
crunchbearonline.com

Donut Palace

Stop into Donut Palace for a sweet treat. They've got a variety of donuts and are known for their apple fritters.

123 S Washington St Junction City, KS 66441 785-579-5311

D'z Lounge

Part coffee lounge, part cocktail lounge, D'z Lounge is an eclectic place with a cozy, artsy vibe. Owner Donya Nejad has created a space with a European feel right in downtown Junction City. If you prefer sweeter drinks, try the Royal Rose, and if you're more of a brown liquor fan, the Smoked Old Fashioned is delicious.
714 N Washington St Junction City, KS 66441 215-433-8942

El Patron Dos

Want some authentic Mexican? You can't go wrong at El Patron Dos. Fan favorites are the street tacos with a choice of meat, including al pastor campechana, barbacoa, and tinga. The carne asada entree is amazing, and don't miss their margaritas. You can choose a taijin rim if you prefer. Since this is "Dos," you might be wondering if there's an original El Patron. There is, and it's in Manhattan, KS. The two restaurants are owned by a husband and wife: he runs JC and she runs Manhattan.
836 S Washington St Junction City, KS 66441 785-390-0191
elpatrondos.com

Filamina Provencal

Filamina Provencal (formerly Onolicious Hawaiian BBQ) has been a hit since opening in early 2024. Owner Kuuleialoha Provencal is from Hawaii and brings dishes from her home to Kansas. She's joined by her husband, Henry, who's a retired soldier. Favorite dishes include kalua pig and Musubi.
1634 N Washington St Junction City, KS 66441 785-375-0560

Frost and Flour

Since opening in February 2024, Frost and Flour is the go-to place for ice cream and baked goods. They bake everything in-house, whether it's a cinnamon rolls, cakes, cupcakes and cookies, muffins, or pies. Their ice cream comes from a small-batch producer in Tell City, Indiana.

725 N Washington St Junction City, KS 66441 785-307-7014 frostandflourjc.com

Highwind Brewing

Another spot that made its 2024 debut is Highwind Brewing. Eight families joined forces to buy the Old Waters Hardware Building in 2021, after it had been vacant for 25 years. When their first plan didn't pan out, they decided to open a brewery. Twenty-eight more families would join them. Since opening in February 2024, Highwind Brewing has been a favorite watering hole. You can get a bite to eat from their food hall, featuring two chef-driven spots: Mill Pizza or 726 Bistro.

726 N Washington St Junction City, KS 66441 785-530-6432 highwindbrewing.com

JC's BBQ & Grill

If you don't get barbecue, are you even in Kansas? JC's BBQ & Grill is a full-service sports bar that smokes its own meat. The televisions are abundant and so is the seating. Check out the brisket nachos or one of their Wagyu burgers. This is one of the few restaurants open daily.

812 E Chestnut St Junction City, KS 66441 785-579-6606
jcbbqgrill.com

Milford Tropics

Feel like you've taken a trip to the Keys at this quirky place complete with tiki bar vibes and mermaid murals. It's a favorite for anglers, with affordable bar food and inexpensive drinks.
103 11th St, Milford, KS 66514 785-463-5551

Paradox Coffee

Start your day off right with a visit to Paradox Coffee and Bistro. This charming spot is as local as they come, even down to the custom wood countertops. The coffee is from Reverie Roasters and dairy products are from Hildebrand Farms. If you're in need of a pick-me-up but don't want coffee, you can get a Lotus Energy Refresher. They offer a variety of sandwiches, paninis, and baked goods. There are several options for seating that are ideal for conversations, including comfy chairs by the fireplace.
419 N Washington St., Junction City, KS 785-209-3809
paradoxcoffeeandbistro.com

Stacy's Restaurant

If you're in the mood for down-home cooking, head to Grandview Plaza and this Geary County staple. Stacy's Restaurant has been serving up comfort food since 1969. It's a local favorite and if you go there more than once during your visit, you'll probably see some return faces. A true measure of a diner is its biscuits and gravy, and these definitely make the grade.
118 W Flint Hills Blvd Junction City, KS 66441 785-238-3039

Thomas' Taste of Chicago

No place does hot dogs, Italian beef, gyros, and Polish sausages like Chicago... unless it's Thomas' Taste of Chicago. A former resident of the Windy City who moved to Junction City when his brother was stationed at Fort Riley, Thomas brings Kansans a bit of his home town. The gyro tastes like it came from Greektown and Thomas says the Chicago Burger is the best in town. Oh, and notice that 773 phone number? That tells you he's bona fide.
105 W 7th St. Junction City, KS 66441 773-790-1713

Tokyo Japanese Restaurant

If you're craving sushi, Tokyo Japanese has an epic list of maki. They've got regular rolls like California, Yellowtail, or Salmon and Avocado and a whole page of special rolls. For non-fans of raw fish, there's also a healthy selection of tempura, teriyaki, fried rice, and noodles. For a fun appetizer, try the stuffed jalapenos, which are open faced and filled with cheese and topped with crunchy tempura, eel sauce, spicy mayo, and green onions.
308 E Chestnut St Junction City, KS 66441 785-579-5151

2 Peaches

If you're in the mood for fried catfish, rice and gravy, or shrimp and grits or other soul food, 2 Peaches has you covered.
431 W 18th St. Junction City, KS 66441 785-390-0027

Tyme Out Steakhouse

Some bars put dollar bills all over their walls and ceiling. At Tyme Out Steakhouse, it's Crown Royal bags. Thousands of them. A Grandview Plaza staple since 1992, they're known for their steaks, and don't miss the garlic butter. You'll also want to check their Facebook page for specials. Why's it spelled like that? The owner's name is Ty.

101 Continental Dr. Junction City, KS 66441 785-238-7638
facebook.com/TymeOutSteakhouse

Food Trucks

10th Street Deli Bulgogi Box

118 N Washington St., JC

The Best Hamburger

113 E Vine St., JC 620-391-8774

By Yurii's Pizza

901 N Washington St., JC 973-610-9057

Cynthia's One Bite Delight

203 S Washington St., JC 785-492-5614

Filos Foods

901 N Washington St., JC 816-550-7623

La Hacienda on Wheels

901 N Washington St., JC 785-200-7530

Pineapple Whip Kansas (May-Sept)

741 W 6th St., JC 479-263-8821

Taste of India

901 N Washington St., JC 785-770-6466

Yumi Hibachi and Sushi

904 W 6th St., JC 785-253-5101

Annual
Events

Annual Events

March

- **Taste of Culture** – A food event that showcases the diversity of Junction City, featuring various international cuisines.

May to October

- **Main Street Market** – A seasonal farmers market held downtown Junction City on Saturdays.

June

- **Paint the Town Blue** – Held in early June to raise awareness and support for law enforcement.

July

- **Freedom Fest** – This multi-day Independence Day celebration features concerts, fireworks, and family-friendly activities.

October

- Oktoberfest – Two days of family fun celebrating German culture and heritage.

- **Boos and Brews** – A fall event blending craft beer with Halloween-themed festivities.

November

- **Wine & Wassail Walk** – A holiday-themed event in downtown Junction City.

December

- **Hometown Christmas** – Celebrates the holiday season with parades, lights, and festive activities.

Extend
Your Trip

Extend Your Trip

Places to Go Beyond Geary County

AFTER SOAKING IN GEARY County, why not see what else is nearby? The region is filled with outdoor adventures, historical landmarks, and unique experiences.

Abilene, Kansas

About 30 minutes west of Geary County

Step back in time in Abilene, boyhood home of President Dwight D. Eisenhower. Visit his presidential library and museum, take a nostalgic ride on the Abilene & Smoky Valley Railroad, or explore the Old West at Old Abilene Town. Don't miss the Greyhound Hall of Fame for a unique experience.

Wamego, Kansas

About 40 minutes northeast of Geary County

Follow the yellow brick road to Wamego, home of the Oz Museum. This charming town also boasts the historic Columbian Theatre and a delightful city park with a mini-train. Visit in October for the annual OZtoberFest celebration.

Topeka, Kansas

About 1 hour east of Geary County

As the capital city of Kansas, Topeka offers a blend of history and culture. Tour the majestic Kansas State Capitol, stroll through the NOTO Arts District, or enjoy family fun at Gage Park and the Topeka Zoo. History buffs will appreciate the Brown v. Board of Education National Historic Site.

Salina, Kansas

About 1 hour northwest of Geary County

Salina offers a mix of culture and family fun. Explore the Rolling Hills Zoo, delve into local history at the Smoky Hill Museum, or cool off at Kenwood Cove Aquatic Park. Art enthusiasts will enjoy the Salina Art Center, while aviation buffs shouldn't miss the Yesteryear Museum.

Tallgrass Prairie National Preserve

About 1 hour southeast of Geary County

Tallgrass Prairie National Preserve protects one of the last remaining areas of tallgrass prairie in North America. This 10,894-acre preserve offers visitors a glimpse into the ecosystem that once covered 170 million acres of the continent, showcasing native grasses, diverse wildlife, and historic structures from the area's ranching past.

Concordia, Kansas

About 1.5 hours northwest of Geary County

Discover a unique piece of American history at Concordia's National Orphan Train Complex. The town also boasts the beautiful Brown Grand Theatre and the Cloud County Historical Museum. For outdoor enthusiasts, nearby Jamestown Wildlife Area offers excellent birdwatching opportunities.

Where to Stay

Where to Stay

GEARY COUNTY MAY BE small, but it does have a variety of places to stay. There are several chain hotels as well as a full-blown camping resort. Below you'll find many of these accommodations. For more options, check out visitgearycounty.com.

Featured: Acorns Resort

Acorns Resort, located on the shores of Milford Lake, is a popular destination for outdoor enthusiasts and families seeking a mix of adventure and relaxation. It offers a range of accommodations, from rustic cabins to spacious lodge rooms and RV campsites, catering to different types of travelers. Visitors can enjoy activities like boating, fishing, hiking, and swimming, with easy access to Milford Lake's pristine waters. The resort also features a full-service marina, making it convenient for those looking to rent boats or dock their own.

For those who prefer to stay on land, Acorns Resort has well-maintained hiking trails, beautiful lake views, and opportunities for wildlife observation. The on-site Cove Bar & Grill is perfect for casual dining, offering a menu with local favorites and seasonal specialties. Bonus: they serve farm-to-table elk meat, and is one of the few places where that's available.

What makes Acorns Resort particularly appealing is its ability to blend a relaxing lakeside atmosphere with modern amenities. The resort is also a prime location for events like weddings and corporate retreats, thanks to its scenic backdrop and flexible spaces. Whether you're an avid angler, a weekend camper, or just someone looking for a peaceful getaway, Acorns Resort is an ideal base for exploring Milford Lake and the surrounding region.

This combination of accommodations, recreational options, and natural beauty makes Acorns Resort a must-visit spot in Geary County for both locals and tourists. It embodies the outdoor charm and hospitality of Kansas, drawing visitors year-round.

Key Features:

- **Scenic Location:** Situated directly on Milford Lake, Acorns Resort offers stunning water views and easy access to various lake activities.

- **Rustic Accommodations:** The resort's log cabins and

rooms provide a rustic and cozy atmosphere, perfect for a relaxing getaway.

- **Lakefront Amenities:** Enjoy swimming, fishing, boating, and other water activities directly from the resort's private beach and boat docks.

- **Peaceful Atmosphere:** Acorns Resort is ideal for those seeking a quiet and serene environment, away from the hustle and bustle of city life.

3710 Farnum Creek Rd, Milford, KS 66514 785-463-4000
acornsresortkansas.com

Additional places to stay:

Best Western J.C. Inn
Conveniently located hotel offering modern amenities like free breakfast and an indoor pool.
604 E Chestnut St, Junction City, KS 66441 785-210-1212
bestwestern.com

Candlewood Suites Junction City - Ft. Riley
Extended-stay hotel offering in-room kitchens and a fitness center.
100 S Hammons Dr, Junction City, KS 66441 785-238-1454
ihg.com

Comfort Inn & Suites Junction City
Offering free breakfast and an indoor pool, located close to Fort Riley.
120 N East St, Junction City, KS 66441 785-762-4200
choicehotels.com

Sonesta Essentials Junction City
A modern hotel featuring a fitness center and on-site dining, ideal for both business and leisure travelers.
310 Hammons Dr, Junction City, KS 66441 785-210-1500
sonesta.com

Econo Lodge
Budget accommodation offering free breakfast and pet-friendly rooms.
211 W Flint Hills Blvd, Junction City, KS 66441 785-238-8181
choicehotels.com

Express Inn & Suites
Budget hotel with complimentary breakfast and an outdoor pool, located near major highways.
1214 S Washington St, Junction City, KS 66441 785-579-6464

Flagstop Resort & RV Park
Located near Milford Lake, this resort offers RV parking, camping, and cabin rentals.
302 Whiting, Milford, KS 66514 785-463-5537
flagstopresort.com

Grandview Plaza Inn & Suites
A simple, budget-friendly option offering free breakfast and Wi-Fi.
110 E Flint Hills Blvd, Junction City, KS 66441 785-579-6987
grandviewplazainnhotel.com

Great Western Inn
A no-frills hotel with free parking and Wi-Fi. Pet-friendly.
201 Continental Dr, Junction City, KS 66441 785-238-5147
N/A

Hampton Inn Junction City
Modern hotel offering complimentary breakfast, free Wi-Fi, a fitness center, and an indoor pool.
1039 S Washington St, Junction City, KS 66441 785-579-6950
hilton.com

Holiday Inn Express & Suites Junction City
Hotel with an indoor pool and complimentary breakfast.
221 E Ash St, Junction City, KS 66441 785-579-5787
ihg.com

Homestead Motel
Small, affordable motel with basic amenities for a short stay.
1736 N Washington St, Junction City, KS 66441 785-238-2886

Motel 6 Junction City
Economy hotel featuring basic rooms, free Wi-Fi, and pet-friendly policies.
1931 Lacy Dr, Junction City, KS 66441 785-762-2215
motel6.com

Quality Inn Junction City
Mid-range hotel offering a free hot breakfast and access to an indoor pool.
305 E Chestnut St, Junction City, KS 66441 785-784-5106
choicehotels.com

Super 8 by Wyndham Junction City
Budget hotel with complimentary breakfast and a convenient location near I-70.
1133 S Washington St, Junction City, KS 66441 785-530-5961
wyndhamhotels.com

USA Inn

A straightforward motel providing free parking and Wi-Fi, located close to Fort Riley.

211 W Flint Hills Blvd, Junction City, KS 66441 785-238-8101

WoodSpring Suites Junction City

Extended-stay hotel offering kitchenettes in every room and free Wi-Fi.

311 E Ash St, Junction City, KS 66441 785-762-2221
woodspring.com

Plan Your Adventure

Plan Your Adventure

READY TO PLAN YOUR trip to Geary County? These planning pages will help you stay organized and keep all your information in one place. There are also journal pages at the back so you can record your memories.

To print these and find even more planning pages, including daily schedule and daily budget, visit *thelocaltourist.com/geary-plann ing*

Included:

- Pre-Trip Checklist

- Accommodations Research Worksheet

- Attractions Research Worksheet

- Restaurants Research Worksheet

- Itinerary

- Attractions

- Restaurants

- Budget

PRE-TRIP CHECKLIST

- ⬡ Book accommodations
- ⬡ Book attractions
- ⬡ Make restaurant reservations
- ⬡ Let someone know about trip: _____
- ⬡ Arrange plant care: _____
- ⬡ Arrange pet care: _____
- ⬡ Share itinerary with: _____
- ⬡ Share location with : _____
- ⬡ Print itinerary & confirmation numbers
- ⬡ Put lights on a timer
- ⬡ Program thermostat
- ⬡ Put mail and paper on hold
- ⬡ Clean out refrigerator/freezer
- ⬡ Put small item on cup of ice
- ⬡ Create ice block(s) for cooler
- ⬡ Take out trash
- ⬡ Lock windows and doors
- ⬡ Unplug small appliances
- ⬡ Get vehicle inspected
- ⬡ Download music, etc.
- ⬡ Download apps
- ⬡ Set up auto-backup for phone
- ⬡ Check for tolls
- ⬡ Map route
- ⬡ Paper maps

NOTES

ACCOMMODATIONS RESEARCH

Write down your potential accommodations and list their estimated costs, pros, and cons.

Accommodations	$$	Pros	Cons

ATTRACTIONS RESEARCH

Write down potential attractions, activities, museums, etc. and list their estimated costs, pros, and cons.

Attractions	$$	Pros	Cons

RESTAURANTS RESEARCH

Write down potential restaurants and dining options and list their estimated costs, pros, and cons.

Restaurants	$$	Pros	Cons

BUDGET

Trip Budget: _____   Total Spent: _____

Transportation	Budget	Actual	+/-
Gas			
Vehicle - rental or maintenance			
Tolls			
Misc			
TOTAL			

Accommodations	Budget	Actual	+/-
TOTAL			

Meals & Activities	Budget	Actual	+/-
Food & Drink			
Activities & Attractions			
Souvenirs			
Misc			
TOTAL			

Pre-trip Expenses	Budget	Actual	+/-
TOTAL			

Notes

ITINERARY

From: _____ To: _____

ACCOMMODATIONS

NAME _____ PHONE _____

ADDRESS _____

WEBSITE _____ CONFIRMATION _____

Day _____ Date _____

Day _____ Date _____

Day _____ Date _____

Day _____ Date _____

ITINERARY

Day _____   Date _____

Day _____   Date _____

Day _____   Date _____

Day _____   Date _____

Day _____   Date _____

Day _____   Date _____

ATTRACTIONS RESEARCH

Write down potential attractions, activities, museums, etc. and list their estimated costs, pros, and cons.

Attractions	$$	Pros	Cons

RESTAURANTS

Name _____ Phone _____ Date _____

Address _____ Reservation _____

Website _____

Notes

Name _____ Phone _____ Date _____

Address _____ Reservation _____

Website _____

Notes

Name _____ Phone _____ Date _____

Address _____ Reservation _____

Website _____

Notes

Name _____ Phone _____ Date _____

Address _____ Reservation _____

Website _____

Notes